CW00557018

*T*ouched *by the G*oddess

Deane Juhan thinks and writes with an incomparable fusion of poetry, passion, hands-on experience, and scientific precision. Now, in *Touched by the Goddess,* an appropriate partner for *Job's Body,* he turns his prolific brilliance to his favorite subjects, arguably the most important issues of our times. The results inspire and enlighten. Deane's writings contribute profoundly to our evolution as a species, and to the medicine of the future that is now upon us. Major pieces of this evolution and of this new medicine emerge from Deane Juhan's thoughtful and heartful exploration of the living substance in those who are fortunate to experience his skilled touch. Here you will find abundant 'food for thought' for everyone, from the medical researcher to the poet or philosopher. For those who use their hands to nourish their fellow beings, Deane's writings continue to be a source of priceless and practical insights into the miracles of life and healing in all of their dimensions.

JAMES OSCHMAN, PH.D.

author of *Energy Medicine: The Scientific Basis*

Deane Juhan, one of the most brilliant bodyworkers of our time, has written a fascinating new book which argues that body-work is a social and spiritual force whose benefits extend well beyond relaxation and rehabilitation. I recommend it to all body-work practitioners, their clients, and anyone who really wants to be inspired about the seemingly endless potential of new paradigm healing.

CANDACE B. PERT, PH.D.

author of *Molecules of Emotion: The Science behind Mind-body Medicine*

THE PHYSICAL, PSYCHOLOGICAL, & SPIRITUAL POWERS OF

BODYWORK

Touched *by the* Goddess

DEANE JUHAN

BARRYTOWN
STATION HILL

Copyright 1994, 1995, 1996, 2002 by Deane Juhan

All rights reserved. No part of this book may be reproduced or utilized in any form or by any means, electronic or mechanical, including photocopying, recording or by any information storage and retrieval system, without permission in writing from the publisher.

Published by Barrytown/Station Hill Press, Inc., Barrytown, NY 12507.
Online catalogue: www.stationhill.org
E-mail: publishers@stationhill.org

Cover by Susan Quasha
Text typesetting Chie Hasegawa

Grateful acknowledgment is due to *Massage Magazine* where the original versions of these essays first appeared between 1994 and 1996 (issues #47-59).

Library of Congress Cataloging-in-Publication Data
Juhan, Deane.
Touched by the Goddess : the physical, psychological, and spiritual powers of bodywork / Deane Juhan.
    p. ; cm.
ISBN 1-58177-081-2
1. Touch—Therapeutic use. 2. Massage.
[DNLM: 1. Therapeutic Touch—Popular Works. 2. Mind-Body and Relaxation Techniques—Popular Works. 3. Spiritual Therapies—Popular Works. WB 890 J93t 2002] I. Title.

RZ999 .J844 2002
615.8'22—dc21

2002013147

CONTENTS

Introduction
  BEYOND ALTERNATIVE HEALTH CARE:
    HEALING A CULTURE OUT OF TOUCH   *Xii*

1   THE GODDESS OF BODYWORK   I

2   THE BODY POLITIC   II

3   CELEBRATING HEDONISM AND SELF-ESTEEM   23

4   TOUCH THE CHILDREN   35

5   SOMATIC EDUCATION AND EVOLUTION   47

6   THE VOICES OF ANGELS   59

7   FACILITATED SEGMENTS:
    BIOMECHANICS AND PATHOLOGY   73

8   MUSCLES AND EMOTIONS   85

9   BEYOND THE BRAIN:
    A BODY OF INFORMATION   97

10   THE BREATH OF LIFE   113

11   TOUCH AND TOLERANCE:
    BODYWORK AS A SOCIAL FORCE   123

Introduction

Beyond Alternative Health Care
Healing a Culture Out of Touch

Ever since I became a bodyworker in 1974 I have been riveted by the healing power of touch. After initially experiencing it as a pleasurable way of relaxing and relieving stress, I soon began to realize that it was far more than that. Investigating what was clinically known about the impact of touch on our organism's development led me to write *Job's Body: A Handbook for Bodywork*, an extensive study of our many physiological responses to touch.

During the last few years my sense of the power of touch has undergone another dramatic expansion. Its potency can be applied not only to physiological and psychological problems, but to interpersonal and social ones as well. My expanded sensibilities about these dimensions of healing touch have in turn led me to speculate what positive effects on the muddled relationships, ineffective social institutions, confused cultural values, and competitive spiritual aspirations we witness around us every day.

This collection of essays now in your hands is an extension of this inquiry. They first appeared in *Massage Magazine* during 1994 and 1995. Upon rereading them, I have been struck by the enduring—even heightened—relevance of many of their themes and speculations. Our world is certainly no less troubled, and our culture no less confused about issues critical to our peaceful and productive coexistence. I put them forward with the hope that in some small way they may encourage the revival in our collective lives of the sensually rich, personally gratifying, and therapeutically potent world of educated touch.

Bodywork of many kinds now occupies a firm niche in the arena of alternative and complimentary health care. Individuals in the United States spend more money out-of-pocket on the alternative therapies as a whole than is spent on traditional medical treatment, and there is a growing recognition of the fact that the successful application of many of these sorts of alternative treatments significantly predate "traditional" medicine. Every year new discoveries and techniques are added to this large body of revived knowledge, and indeed the alternative field is currently the fastest expanding sector of our health care system.

This means that there are steadily growing numbers of people among us who are experiencing the palliative and educational effects of bodywork on a more regular basis. In my own professional community and among my own students and clients I have watched the emergence of wonderful latent personal qualities, a deepening (or even a birth) of tolerance and respect between individuals, moments of tremendous interpersonal insight together, and the kind of collective cohesion that encourages safety, mutual trust and support, constructive risk taking, honesty in expression and authenticity in action.

All of these developments are quite above and beyond any specific physical or emotional healing that is taking place in my sessions and classes, and they are increasingly focusing my interest. If these kinds of interpersonal effects operate on the small scale of sessions and classes, then their transference to larger and larger arenas may be entirely possible. And this would be a very good thing indeed.

What might be the cumulative effects of more and more individuals literally more "in touch" with their bodies, their lives and each other? What would a society look like, feel like, where a general suppression of nurturing contact was not the price to be paid for avoiding abuse, where it was understood that an adequate amount of touch is necessary to the health—and even the survival—of children, elders, sick people, lonely people, troubled people, people at large? What might it feel like on buses or sidewalks, in gatherings large and small, where people were more skilled in quiet boundary negotiations, tolerant deference to the rhythms and style of others, supportive touches, helpful touches, consoling touches, and a mutual common concern that transcends their families and personal relationships? What pains and pitfalls of courtship and marriage might be avoided altogether if partners knew how to touch each other in genuinely supportive and gratifying ways? How might the rewards of parenting and the experiences of childhood be enhanced by parents who understand that the physical, emotional and intellectual robustness of all children rests as decisively upon their receiving enough nourishing touch as it does upon any other input or training? In short, what kind of a social world might evolve if nourishing, pleasuring, gratifying touch were both safe and readily available, and where the deep human needs addressed by that touch were more valued and more consistently met?

Touch as Food

The central galvanizing discovery for me when I was reading the clinical literature that led to *Job's Body* was the startling fact that no infant mammal can survive without enough tactile input. Zoo keepers and farmers have long been aware of this, and have conscientiously supplied that input if the mother could not. But there was very little awareness of such a thing in the general population, and the principle was certainly not applied in any systematic way to infant care and child-rearing in our culture.

It was not until extraordinarily high mortality rates of infants in orphanages (around 98%!) in the nineteenth century were investigated that the decisive role of touch for infant survival was recognized. These children were fed and sheltered, but handled minimally by overworked and understaffed institutions. When an inspired researcher added enough staff in one orphanage so that periods of affectionate fondling and interacting could be added to each infant's regimen, that mortality rate plummeted to normal averages and the children thrived.

Later laboratory studies that isolated infant mammals confirmed that they all died of similar causes: eruptions of bladders or bowels. If the mother's tongue, or some caretaker's swab, did not stroke the new infant's skin, the infants were powerless to void these organs. In a word, they require tactile jumpstarting. Without the tactile stimulation, the autonomic reflexes are not initiated and established; without receiving sensation, the infants' nervous systems could not locate and operate crucial muscles.

Further surveys of human subjects revealed a whole continuum of deformities and maladaptations that hinge upon the amount of touch children received throughout their growth and development. Those that have received enough to survive their infancy, but no more, develop a spectrum of deformities called "deprivation dwarfism": stunted growth, misshapen skulls, distorted rib cages, crooked limbs, along with severe cognitive and emotional difficulties. The absence of enough touching actually subverts the successful expression of their genes. It is significant that these impairments mimic those of severe malnutrition during childhood. Touch for children is clearly a crucial form of nourishment, as important as food, water, or oxygen.

If a little more touch is available during growth, these severe physical distortions are prevented, but serious cognitive and emotional difficulties persist. More touch than that and these psychological symptoms manifest less and less severely, finally not manifesting at all for individuals who have had all the touching they required for their healthy development.

These kinds of conditions and results have been demonstrated repeatedly with a wide variety of laboratory animals. One of the most arresting extended experiments was one conducted by Harry Harlow, dubbed "Harlow's Monkeys." Infant monkeys were isolated from their mothers and given two kinds of surrogate mother: A cold wire-frame figure that dispensed milk from a baby bottle, and one that had been covered with soft terry cloth and warmed with an interior light bulb but with no milk source. Harlow's theoretical assumption was that the warm cuddly mother figure would prove to be more attractive more of the time than the cold hard one with the food. What he did not anticipate was the overwhelming strength of that preference.

The infant monkeys would spend far more time with the cuddly figure, typically going to the wire one only as long as necessary to feed, and then hopping back into the other's soft warm lap. Some of them would even under-nourish themselves for the sake of their preference for the pleasuring and the sense of security unavailable from the wire food source.

Furthermore, monkeys that were given only the wire-bottle figure all exhibited extreme psychological problems and pathological behaviors as they grew. They huddled in a corner of their cage, mute and motionless for long stretches between hurried feeding episodes. They did not learn tasks well, or even interact with their handlers normally. They did not socialize with other monkeys if given the opportunity. If a strange object was placed in their cage their response was not curiosity, not even cautious curiosity, but either frightened hysterical withdrawal or exaggerated defensive postures that were sustained until the strange object was removed.

It would be hard to imagine a more dramatic demonstration of these young primates' instinctual need for tactile nourishment and support for their healthy development. And there can be no doubt that their responses reinforce the notion that all mammals, ourselves very much included, absolutely require these conditions in order to thrive.

Touch as Language

All these observations, and many more that have reinforced the robustness of the theory, are testaments to the necessity of touch for normal physiological and psychological development. What I have been fascinated with more lately are the implications of this information for human relations of all kinds, from our subjective relationship with our own bodies, to interpersonal relationships, larger social units and finally the culture as a whole.

Many of the chronic physiological problems and maladaptive behaviors evidenced by the stressed lab animals are very reminiscent of behaviors commonly observable in homes, schools, workplaces and communities. Children who are undernourished in this particular way tend to either withdraw into isolation or become unruly in an attempt to secure attention. This in turn generates social interactions that are far from optimal and that negatively condition these lives in an ever-increasing number of ways.

Such children tend to go on to become adults who have a muted capacity for self-awareness, self-regulation, personal intimacy, and generally adaptive responses to the naturally changing conditions of their lives. This is what I mean when I say "out of touch," and it leads to dangerous situations in which individuals are more vulnerable to chronic degenerative illness, chronic stress, depression, impaired performance—the growing list of developmental illnesses and dysfunctions that are becoming more and more prevalent in our society. And it further leads to social interactions that are continually haunted and disrupted by some measure of the psychological distress displayed by Harlow's monkeys and that increasingly become motivated by the ache and the rage of deep needs unmet. It is a common observation in primate studies that apes who groom one another the most often are the ones that are the least likely to express hostility to one another. Is it unreasonable to speculate that the kind of damage caused by insufficient friendly physical contact may well underlie much of the violence in our culture that so far has eluded explanation or remedy?

One component of the positive effect of touch appears to be the stimulation of normal autonomic and skeletomuscular reflexes, the sensory "jump start." But another dimension of what makes the lucky infants thrive seems to be educational—information is being received about a great many important things through the medium of touch. Indeed, the scope of the information that is exchanged through touching is so vast and so detailed that we have to speak of *the language of touch*.

Physical contact, and the flow of interpersonal impressions that arise from it, generate a whole world of non-verbal, preverbal information and intelligence. Furthermore, this silent language is far older than the spoken or written word, and is shared in common across cultural and spoken language barriers the world over. And it communicates impressions that often have no immediate counterpart in verbal language. Frequently, in fact, the intention or personality of another person that I perceive directly through touch is at odds with their words and facial expressions. William Faulkner stated it powerfully:

> Because there is something in the touch of flesh with flesh which abrogates, cuts sharp and straight across the devious intricate channels of decorous ordering, which enemies as well as lovers know because it makes them both—touch and touch of that which is the citadel of the central I-am's private own: not spirit, soul; the liquorish and ungirdled mind is anyone's to take in any darkened hallway of this earthly tenement. But let flesh touch with flesh, and watch the fall of all the egg-shell shibboleth of caste and color too.
>
> *(Absalom, Absalom)*

There is something in the experience of touch that is not merely sensory, but that is potentially revelatory as well.

To the degree that we have learned to do so, we all instinctually communicate with this language of touch in a wide variety of ways. Something as simple as a handshake reveals much about the character and the current mood of both participants, which is one of the principle reasons that it has endured as an initial gesture of meeting and greeting. And there are hands held affectionately, loving caresses, punishing slaps, pats on the back or on the back of the hand, calming stokes, threatening jabs, reassuring squeezes, hugs of hello, hugs of good-bye, and on and on.

These kinds of examples are what might be called *the vocabulary of interpersonal contact*, the commonly shared meanings of specific conventions of touching. But just as in written language, this collection of conventional meanings is only the beginning of the possible depths of communication and mutual learning. The more we make contact with individuals, the more we realize that the manner in which they make these gestures generates a completely different stream of information about each of them, and about ourselves in relation to them. Beyond a vocabulary, there is a tonal dimension to touching, a direct embodiment and reception of qualities that are continually lurking beneath the skin, unspoken. Cumulative physical contacts with people builds for us a growing impression of who and what they are that goes far beyond what we learn from their words. Indeed, we cannot really "take someone at their word" before we have established enough non-verbal impressions concerning their intentions and authenticity. This is what used to be called "getting vibes."

Perhaps the richest source of touching for many people is their relationships with animals, either as farmers, trainers or pet owners. An elaborate communication evolves with animals just as it does between humans, and complex relationships are formed with no common language but touch to inform them. This context of interacting with animals points to a special dimension of this preverbal language. The communicative power of touch cuts across more than "the barriers of caste and color too." It is trans-species, and it connects many different kinds of animals to one another in ways that are recognizably similar from one species to another. And it also connects us to many other kinds of creatures in elaborate and mutually meaningful ways. No relationship can develop until there is mutual knowledge about each other, and our relationships with the mute animals speaks volumes to the power of this alternate way of speaking.

Now, our culture to a large degree has come to regard "language," and even "intelligence," as the ability to manipulate various kinds of signs and symbols—words, numbers, formulas, images, and so on—and to accurately interpret them. This is primarily what education in our society focuses on, and so it is the only intelligence that "counts." But to the degree that we focus exclusively on the information developed by the written and spoken forms of human language—which are marvelous and indeed a domain of intelligence that is ours alone—we ignore to our impoverishment whole realms of information, negotiation strategies and adaptive solutions that are the *lingua franca* of the rest of the animal kingdom.

Nature is not dominated by ruthless competition, "red in tooth and claw," so much as it is bustling with exchanges, ritualized threats and reconciliations, boundary negotiations, the evolving of hierarchies of social relations within groups and between groups, and a wealth of other interactions that keeps every niche in a more or less stable and relatively safe cooperative state. Posture, gesture, and physical contact make up a great deal of the vocabulary, grammar, and public record of these encounters and arrangements.

We have been educated in ways that ignore the collective wisdom of these "merely instinctual" behaviors. There are serious biologists who still maintain that no "lower" life form is endowed with intelligence at all. This definition of intelligence and meaningful purpose as exclusively human traits has serious negative consequences, quite apart from the unpleasant egotistical posturing that it fosters. It limits our focus to the only kind of intelligence that is exclusively human, and so cuts us off from any direct contact with the many other forms of intelligence that have evolved in all creatures since the beginning of biology.

To be sure, the intellect is a wonderful thing in many respects, and a well-trained one is more powerful than one that is not. Illiteracy is the cause of severe limitations. But growing numbers of learning theorists are recognizing that intelligence comes in many forms, that learning takes place in many ways and that there are a corresponding number of illiteracies. For instance, Antonio Damasio is a neurologist who has developed the concept of an "emotional IQ"—how acutely we are able to consciously experience our feelings, understand what they are trying to tell us, and respond to them effectively. It turns out that the successful management of our emotional states has a great deal to do with learning, recall, and performance of all kinds, that and this involves a completely different sort of "intelligence." Therefore our emotional reactions are not something that needs to be left at the door if we are to enter into a scientific understanding of things. They are themselves part of the data of biological processes that need to be accounted for.

The Case for Touch IQ

We have recognized these two domains of intellect and emotions' in a crude way, and one that has been none too helpful to our society. Throughout most of our history we have assigned the intellect primarily to men and the world of feelings to women. These "specialties" have largely been culturally determined and enforced, with the effect that neither gender understands or thinks all that highly of the other.

"Men are from Mars, women are from Venus ."

Touch can function as a bridge across this gulf of misunderstanding and mistrust. The sensations that are produced generate information, while the specific qualities of those sensations are evocative of feelings. Touch partakes of both domains, or perhaps more accurately, it sets in motion a larger, inclusive domain in which thoughts and feelings are equal players in a healthy and balanced organism.

Many beliefs, conventions, and mores in our culture contrive to keep us out of touch with our bodies and our feelings in the immediate and literal sense of the word. Our creative imaginations have served us powerfully, and more and more we are pulled up into the cognitive and rational world which that imagination inhabits. More and more we learn to dwell in a "virtual reality" that has less and less to do with the actual biological needs of the organism that produces it. And worse, we become so immersed in that virtual reality that we often fail to anticipate—or even to notice after the fact—the dire consequences that many of the products of that inventive imagination turn out to have upon ourselves, those around us, and the environment as a whole. With many of the issues I am addressing here, we are not as much in a state of ignorance or denial as in a state of utter distraction.

This muddle is becoming increasingly menacing, and I have come to believe that these very issues are at the heart of the matter in our dislocated and troubled world. When we are not in touch with our genuine individual and collective needs, when we do not inhabit our sensory experiences intimately enough to accurately assess those needs, and when there are few contexts in which they can be fully met, then anxiety, isolation and dysfunctional behavior become more prevalent and problematical. And the problems that arise as a result are certainly not effectively addressed by the damage control that pharmacology or surgery provide.

The histories of the industrial, scientific and technical revolutions demonstrate that our inventive intellects are just as apt to create more efficient destructiveness as anything else—unless the heart is as consciously cultivated as the intellect, unless feeling is as valued as thinking, and unless we are in intimate contact with consequences.

We cannot hope that an industrialist will ever understand what he is doing to the Ohio River until he comes to understand what he is doing to his own blood stream. It is my conviction that bodywork—the conscious development of touch

IQ—can help bring much to bear in the sorting out of these dangerous insensitivities and damaging gaps in our awareness of ourselves and the world. Just as we required touch in infancy to survive, we require it throughout our lives in order to continually improve, or even to simply maintain, the quality of that survival and to continue to adapt to changing circumstances that constantly challenge our previous solutions and habits. We require it to be in full possession of ourselves and our lives.

Bodywork has come of age over the last century or so primarily as an adjunct to health care and rehabilitation. Quite naturally in this context, much emphasis has been placed on "fixing" things. And in fact a great many problems have been "fixed" with bodywork, problems that were not responsive to mainstream medical treatment. And of course I am thrilled every time a client reports a chronic pain alleviated, a healing process accelerated, a limitation resolved. This is the physiology of touch and the biomechanics of the organism, the things that absorbed me in the writing of *Job's Body,* and genuine contributions that hands-on therapies have to offer to the healing arts.

But it has come to be far more than that for me. Bodywork puts us directly in touch with biological intelligence at work in a living creature, and places us in the midst of their processes of learning and adaptive change with our focus heightened. It exposes us to all of the forms of intelligence that sustain all creatures. And from these vantage points emerges a whole new appreciation of how the critter works in all its dimensions.

And even beyond that, it plunges both participants into a world of mutually shared and verifiable subjective experience, and helps more than anything I know to recover those inner sensibilities that have been so damaged and crippled by the tyranny of the "objective" in virtually all of our learning experiences. And as these mutual subjective realities become clearer and stronger, and are shared by more and more people, a whole new sense of self, a much bigger sense of self and interconnectedness begins to emerge. A sense of common purpose and mutual need arrives, that practical yet mystical union E. M. Forster was referring to with his motto, "Only connect."

For all its uniqueness and power, our intellect is simply not enough to maintain our health and sustain our survival. The world of sensations and feelings is not there to be either neurotically suppressed or hedonistically titillated and indulged. This world springs to life within us to teach us, to guide us, it announces changes that have happened or that need to happen in order to let us know when all is well and to help us anticipate what is next. And even beyond putting us in touch with our authentic feelings, compassionate touch has the power to form deep bonds based upon mutual need and mutual gratification. It is a resource that has been grievously devalued by our culture, and its absence may well be largely responsible for the many kinds of pain and limitation that manifest themselves on so many levels of our coexistence.

I

The Goddess of Bodywork

A rapid and exciting crystallization is occurring within the bodywork profession. The number of those seeking training and certification is growing exponentially. Alternative health care modalities are beginning to attract the interest of research facilities and government funding agencies. These are heady days indeed for those who have been working for decades in relative obscurity.

But this crystallization is not without its attendant anxieties. All such processes are fragile and uncertain in their initial stages, and as previously invisible elements precipitate into enduring structures, some decidedly undesirable characteristics may solidify into permanent shapes as well. Some state and local lawmakers are making genuine attempts to responsibly recognize, select, and include therapeutic massage and other alternative modalities in their licensing and regulatory guidelines; others are simply sweeping all "touchy-feely" approaches into the legal dust-bins of prostitution or unethical counseling practices. Some physicians see the $23 billion annually spent out-of-pocket in this country alone for alternative health care treatment as a positive indicator of future health care trends; others see it as a competitive threat that must be stamped out to "protect" the public from "unproven" and presumably fraudulent practices.

And the burgeoning bodywork community is itself in some disarray with regard to national collective issues. Many would prefer to remain in obscurity rather than confront the issues created by publicity, legislative interests, national standards, regulatory controls, and all the rest of it. Small massage schools and professional organizations fear the unspoken competitive agenda and potential clout of larger, more politically active ones.

Collectively we are only at the most rudimentary stages of a dialogue that would produce a solid conceptual framework and a vocabulary that will allow us to define our common principles and individual differences in a clear and systematic way. In fact, practitioners and teachers in many modalities strongly resist such definition and clarity because they feel that "scientific" analysis of this kind inherently undermines the crucial intuitive and non-verbal foundations of bodywork. Nor is the kind of record-keeping that generates scientifically meaningful data common practice among bodyworkers.

Modern medicine, with its emphasis on clinical research, pharmacology, surgery, and technology, has come to dominate health care because its successes have been dramatic, easy to see, and simple to understand in lay terms. Its practitioners have common goals, common vocabulary, and common procedures for both research and application. They work, for the most part, with a common purpose, one which they have all learned to define in similar and consistent terms. They are all animated by a common *archetype*, and they gather their efforts under a common icon—the serpent and the staff.

The serpent and the staff belonged to Asclepius, the Greek god of medicine, and his purview has changed little over the centuries. He is the *combatant of disease*, and his genius lies in the use of objective analysis to identify diseases, differentiate them from one another, and seek a specific cure for each specific condition. In his view these diseases are autonomous agents caused primarily by germs, viruses, toxins, or genetic flaws, and his method of attack is the categorization of causes, organs affected, nature of the disturbance, observable symptoms and carefully defined therapies to which they respond. His role, embodied by the physician, is to *intervene* between the patients and their diseases, with the view that once the disease is vanquished the patient will again be restored to normal health. He is the defender of the periphery, the aggressor against threatening incursions, a biological policeman. And of course, he is male, and has a special authority based upon special knowledge and expertise. He is a powerful and compelling deity, with many magnificent temples, dedicated priests and priestesses, and countless beneficiaries.

But Asclepius traditionally had a female counterpart—a colleague, a daughter, or in later versions a wife—who actively represented the *other* side of human developmental and physiological concerns. She was Hygieia, the *goddess of health*. Our oblations to her, and even our understanding of her scope and power, have been in a long decline. Naturally, we run to Asclepius when we are seriously injured or ill, and we give thankful homage when we are cured of our symptoms. But we have forgotten that health is something more than the absence of active disease. It is not a neutral, impersonal, self-sustaining state of static balance; it is a continual process of growth, learning, change, adaptation, compensation, and improvement. Unlike a cure, health has no clearly defined goal; it is open-ended, eternally unfinished, constantly challenged by changing conditions, always creating new levels of optimum performance and pleasure.

These blessings of Hygieia, while they are a birthright, do not fall into our passive laps. They have to be sought. The workings of the goddess have their own laws, their own disciplines, their own necessary ingredients, and their own consequences—all related to but quite different from those of Asclepius. The lifelong cultivation of health does not require aggressive intervention of special expertise of a higher authority; it requires the learning of simple but powerful principles, the nurturing of productive habits, the searching for new solutions to new problems before they *become* pathologies, and—above all—the active and intelligent engagement of the individual in the shaping of a vibrant and productive life. She is not the authority but rather the teacher, not the policeman but the social worker, not the plumber or redecorator, but the housekeeper and the consistent and timely payer of the organic bills. These are the concerns of Hygieia, and our homage to her is simply attending to them.

During our period of modern history when advances in surgery, drugs, and technology have been dramatic and life-saving, the active cultivation of Hygieia has fallen into neglect, while the strengths and appeal of Asclepius have captured the attention and public funding. And Hygiegia's disappearance as an active, vibrant element in our thinking and behaving is directly reflected in the conceptual and logistical gaps in *many* of our institutions—not just those obviously related to health care. Hygieia is the one who reminds us that pathology is a *relationship*—as bio*graphical* as it is bio*logical*—and not merely an intrusion of an autonomous germ. Hers is not a fixed and defined world of dualistic polarities (body/mind, health/disease, living/dying) but rather one of unification, inclusion, and dynamic interaction over time. Her concern is not with the agents of disease per se, but rather with the conditions we have created within and around ourselves which invite them. Hers is an educational and diplomatic, not a military mission.

As unfamiliar as they are to many these days, these principles are scarcely novel. Even Louis Pasteur, one of the fathers of modern pharmaceutical medicine, understood that the proliferation of the most virulent germ requires a supportive environment for its growth, and that "drugs cannot be effective in the long run until steps have been taken to correct the physiological and social conditions originally responsible for the disease." Disease is not something that can be ultimately separated and expunged from nature, because it is itself a natural process. Hygieia's strategy is not to vanquish the enemy—which often tears up a good deal of the native countryside as well as destroying the invaders—but rather to develop a biological context that effectively resists invasion in the first place, and that has strong initial lines of natural defense in the event of exposure.

The principles of Hygieia have been in silent and extraordinarily effective operation, even in the midst of the current ascendancy of Asclepius. In fact, a good many positive overall developments that are usually credited to surgery, drugs, and technology have actually been the result of the quiet, invisible, and largely unnoticed work of Hygieia.

For instance, it has long been assumed that the dramatic drop in infant death rates and rise in life expectancy were largely due to the advent of germ theory and the clinical discovery of specific magic bullets to combat specific kinds of infection. But a closer look at the historical data reveals that both infant death and extended life expectancy began to make their dramatic shifts several generations before germ theory was established. The root causes were improvements in public sanitation practices, the reduction of early forms of industrial pollution, farming and food storage techniques that made fresh and untainted foods available to the public at large, the development of cotton textiles for inexpensive, washable undergarments, and other such advances made long before anyone recognized the existence or understood the mechanisms of the bacteria and the toxins that naturally thrived in unclean surroundings. These sorts of *un*-Hygienic conditions continue to be the primary culprits in impoverished and uneducated populations, even in the presence of antibiotics and vaccinations.

And, in the context of the current controversies about alternative forms of health care, it is well to remember that even after the clinical discovery of germ theory physicians were for a generation almost universally opposed to its more obvious practical applications. Simple sterilization of medicines, instruments, robes, bedding, floors, walls, doorknobs, and so on seemed to be an altogether too troublesome measure to take. And the suggestion that surgeons and physicians take great pains to disinfect themselves before treatment was met with the most umbrage of all— the very idea that they, the experts on disease and cure, could themselves be responsible for illness and death due to their own ignorance and negligence was simply not an idea capable of being seriously entertained. This Hygieia was clearly just another old wive's tale.

What can in truth be said about modern medicine—and this is not small cause for celebration and honor—is that it has been extremely successful in controlling the kinds of diseases that humans have in common with all other mammals; the diseases, that is, which are associated with germs, toxins, genetics, and trauma. Against the diseases that are specifically human—those that are developmental, degenerative, chronic, psychosomatic, functional—the record is not so impressive; indeed is downright dismal. The killers that dominate our mortality statistics these days have nothing to do with germs or traumas. They are heart and cardiovascular conditions, immune system weaknesses and malfunctions, metabolic imbalances, connective tissue pathologies, cancers, peptic ulcers, and other acquired and habituated distortions of homeostasis and other natural processes.

"They are related," in the words of Irvin M. Korr, osteopathic researcher and theorist, "to the anatomic rearrangements associated with verticality and to man's incomplete structural and functional adaptation to the erect stance. The demands of gravity present man with peculiarly difficult biologic 'problems' which are only now beginning to receive systematic investigation. Primarily biomechanical in origin, they are problems in circulation, in distribution of fluids, in drainage of organs, tissues, and cavities, in the mechanical aspects of visceral function, in gestation and parturition, in the secondary effects on cellular function and metabolism and, most particularly, in the massive motor system of the body through which we act on our environment and express our very lives."

These are not problems that can be solved once and for all by any sort of intervention or procedure. They are ongoing developments whose elements and relationships change as we continually create changing circumstances in our growing, maturing, and aging processes. They can be successfully addressed only by self-assessment and self-regulation, active engagement and self-responsibility, the conscious intention to improve internal patterns and functions, and the development of a subjective sensibility that continually guides us towards more favorable operating conditions for the kaleidoscope of biological processes interactive within us. When we are learning these things, and when we are applying their lessons to our own vitality, intelligence, and activity, we are under the effective tutelage of Hygieia, drinking the milk of her nature just as she nourishes the serpent of Asclepius.

It is surely no accident that bodywork as a profession is struggling to come of age and enter the mainstream of American health care at the same time that our current health care system is facing crisis, upheaval, and the need for substantial change. Much has been said, and a great deal of politics played, around the idea of "health care reform."But it is still a shame that even their efforts so far have been concentrated upon tinkering with the economics and logistics of what is currently available within the present system, as though rising costs, unnecessary tests, sloppy management, and redundant paperwork were the only—or even the major—factors preventing the average individual to enjoying improved health and performance.

Our profession has far more profound insights to offer, far more resources to mobilize, and far more cost-effective measures to bring to bear on the chronic and degenerative developmental problems. But the making of this contribution is wholly up to us. We cannot expect government agencies or the AMA to pound our doors in search of solutions that we have not clearly articulated, nor can we expect a public to bring consumer pressure to bear upon alternatives that they neither understand nor trust.

This is why the bodywork profession needs, in one form or another, to resuscitate and re-inhabit Hygieia's archetype, her guidance, her leadership. Common goals, common principles, common vocabulary and a shared sense of values and purpose are the things that lend unity, duration, and force to any collective human enterprise, and it is the special function of apt symbols and personifications to gather apparent differences together into synergistic activity. We now suffer from identification with quite another sort of archetype, that of the "intuitive"—even mystical—shaman-like practitioner, a cherished underdog status, the secret sweetness of esoteric truths and invisible, supernatural forces.

The profession will be much better served in the marketplace of ideas and action if we can remember that we are not engaged in an enterprise that is in any way "unscientific"or opposed to simple and demonstrable axioms. Nothing could create more confusion about our means or be more counterproductive to our ends than to engage in a debate about the values of science versus non-science. Hygieia is, properly speaking, simply the *other side* of medical science, the side which is primarily concerned with examining and redirecting the behavior of the host in the dis-eased relationship.

The fact that it is high time—past time—to resuscitate Hygieia has not completely escaped the notice of potential and powerful allies within the existing establishment. Not long after stepping down from his experience as Physician General, Everett C. Koop concluded that only marginal improvements in life expectancy and life quality were attainable given the current status quo. But if, he went on to say, Americans could somehow simply stop smoking tobacco, drink alcohol in moderation, eat more fresh produce and less fat, and exercise adequately, our national health costs could easily be cut in *half* within a decade.

The clinicians of Asclepius can tell us exactly what it is that is infecting and maiming us. And they can recite the physiology and biochemistry of what would happen if we were to take Dr. Koop's advice. What they appear to be powerless to do is to actually change the public' behavior.

This change does not require convincing scientific studies or dire warnings from voices of authority. What we need are increased sensory awareness for better self-examination, the opportunity to actually feel what it might be like to function better and feel better, and the active awakening of a sense of self-responsibility for the outcome of our actions. Continual *self-engagement* with my organism and its surroundings, and *motivation* to voluntarily adopt positive changes are the keys here. And these are precisely the contributions of Hygieia, nurturer of the serpent.

2

The Body Politic

Nothing is as precious to me as life, no place I know of as marvelous as this planet, and nothing more end- lessly fascinating than its human creatures. More than any other factors, it was the desire to expand my awareness of these riches—to touch them, to grow with them, to experi- ence to the limit their depth and breadth—that led me into my involvement with bodywork and has made every day of it a new challenge and a wonder.

And yet anxiety, skepticism (not to say cynicism), and a flitting, shadowy sense of futility continue to be disturbing and abiding issues for me; there are times when I am not sure that broader and more acute awareness of the human condi- tion is what I really need or want. The daily news does not give me a great deal of reassurance about the security of these riches. On the contrary, it is for the most part the daily ac- counting of the naiveté, fraud, theft, and squandering that point threateningly towards planetary bankruptcy.

Racial, ethnic, and nationalist fears and hatreds appear to be handily unraveling any and all gains from the collapse of the Cold War. Our own "national interest" is so fractured and confused that we can scarcely decide who or whether to invade next or why. On the other hand, our search for a co- herent "domestic policy" is a series of staggering lurches be- tween a "conservative" brand of capitalism that amounts to little more than the legal licensing of the robber barons and a "liberal" bureaucratic and regulatory sort of socialism that effectively stifles self-motivation and prosperity alike.

In this context, what we perceive as a "crime problem" can arguably be viewed as aggressive attempts by the have-nots to secure the kinds of personal security and entrepreneurial advantages enjoyed so ostentatiously—and often with little more moral justification—by the haves.

And in the meantime, explosions of population, production, and profligate waste escalate to engulf us with proliferations as lethal in the long run as the much-feared nuclear one. The fact that the obvious degradations of both local and global environments, there for all to see and feel, can spark what passes for scientific debate is perhaps the most alarming sign of all. This is a chilling indication that important segments of the collective conscious have altogether lost track of the biological and evolutionary rudiments of survival. The very idea that economic growth can proceed indefinitely without due regard to its natural resources is itself the dead canary in the coal mine.

One option, of course, is to simply stop listening to the news. In this way I could preserve my own emotional balance so that I can impart more positive feelings to my clients. This is a fairly common solution among my colleagues, and when I am struggling with my own anger or nausea it appeals mightily to me as well. And yet there are aspects of this withdrawal from negativity that frighten me even more than the various prospects for tomorrow's headlines.

Did we really experience the exhilarations and weather the turbulence of the sixties and seventies just to retreat, intellectually and politically defeated, into the salvaged remains of a fuzzy hedonism and cloistered self-esteem? The name of the mechanism for this self-enforced equanimity is *denial*, and everything that I have learned from bodywork convinces me that the blissful ignorance it protects is very often (perhaps one should say inevitably) more dangerous than the awful truth. "Before the bar of nature and fate," says Jung in *An*

Answer to Job, "unconsciousness is never accepted as an excuse; on the contrary, there are severe penalties for it."

Besides—and this for me is the crucial point—retiring to my treatment room is no escape from the troubling issues. The dysfunctional habits and restrictions of movements, the painful symptoms, the pathologies, and the patterns of compensation that I encounter there are nothing but the physical extensions of my clients' mental states, and these in turn reflect to a high degree their experiences of the social context in which they find themselves. The problems of the individual and the society are no more separable than are those of the body and the mind.

Whatever I have avoided in the headlines I am forced to read in the tissues, and in fact it is here that I most inescapably encounter the crux of many global problems. How can an industrialist understand what his factory is doing to the Mississippi River if he can't even perceive what he is doing to his own bloodstream? What can greater social freedom mean to someone who is imprisoned by their own habits? What is patience to someone who is struggling for their next breath, or flexible negotiations to someone who can't bend over, or tolerance to someone with raw nerves, or honesty to someone who is hiding from their own pain and its very source within themselves, or accountability to someone who will not take personal responsibility for the condition of their own body?

This is why bodywork put me through lasting personal changes and why it appealed to me as a career: Not because it avoided painful social or political problems for which I had no solution, but precisely because it plunged me into the heart of the matter, into the blood and guts of the issues, turned me inside out and exposed the politics in the pit of my stomach. Because it taught me that my body is my only window on the world, my point of view, and that its cleanliness and clarity have everything to do with what I am able to see, which in turn has everything to do with what I believe to be true, which has everything to do with my behavior, which is my only means of changing anything either inside or outside of myself. Because it taught me that my active engagement with my body was the source of any and all solutions that might be brought to bear on my situation—not because my body was the locus of all problems, but because it was my only means of perceiving, understanding, and dealing with any of them. Because it showed me that my body is my personal world, and that the qualities of that world are spun out of the consciousness of my body.

Usually such talk about parallels between "my body, consciousness, and world" is taken to be either mystical or metaphorical. Frequently, however, it can be quite material and literal. Let us consider some of the elements of our political psychology in relation to some of our biological functions, and see if some plausible connections might be found.

In our typical dualistic fashion, we have arranged our contemporary political debates around two great complimentary and opposite poles, which we call *liberal* and *conservative*. These two political camps represent fundamentally different strategies for managing our lives, strategies that emphasize different values, different means and ends, different ideas about the nature of progress and of the social bond. Also typically, we tend to view them as mutually antagonistic, and to assume that one or the other must "win" in order for a coherent political philosophy and a plan of action to successfully emerge and guide our collective lives.

Now every individual and every society is obliged to address two primary concerns: 1) survival, and 2) seeing to it that survival is worth having. And in order both to insure survival and to cultivate well-being, two fundamental mechanisms are required: 1) a means of enforcing the genuinely necessary elements of the *status quo*, of preserving strategies that have worked, culling tried and true principles, of bringing past experience to bear upon present decisions; and 2) a means of seeking out, identifying, assessing, and adapting to *novelty*. Without the former we cannot utilize the lessons of our past to sustain our present, and without the latter we cannot successfully negotiate our future.

Of course the necessary conditions for sheer survival do take precedence in obvious ways, and this fact accounts for both the powerful emotional appeal of *security* and the historical willingness to submit to a rigid *conservatism*. We are driven to these safe havens by the anxiety inherent in our mortality, and to the degree that our anxiety is genuinely resolved by them, nothing could seem wiser than to stay there.

Conservatism usually places great value upon conformity because one of its chief values is *reliability*. It relies on precedent for its principle guidance because it is primarily interested in familiar patterns that have proven to be successful over long periods of time. It tends to enshrine and defer to authority—in politics, education, science, health care, religion, or social conventions, and thus it tends to create and perpetuate hierarchies wherever it thrives. And the more infallible this authority can contrive to appear, the more seemingly reliable is the security which it protects. It is most comfortable within a stable status quo—even a dysfunctional one—as long as the status quo has some measure of staying power, the reasoning being something like, "Life is complex and uncertain. Whatever I am doing, it has worked well enough to get me here. If I change now, perhaps nothing will work at all." When a society at large is entrenched in this line of thinking, substantive change usually requires the motivation of a crisis.

Since job one is to stay alive, a good many of our physiological processes and brain functions are devoted to carefully conserving crucial values. The maintenance of *homeostasis*, for instance, engages the resources of the entire organism in order to continually counterbalance and neutralize any fluctuations in the internal chemical milieu that could be threatening. Temperature, acidity, ionic charge levels, blood sugar levels, and legions of other biochemical relationships must all be held within narrow ranges of balance for life to continue.

Most of these conserving operations are contained deep within the unconscious precincts of the psyche and deep within the protective layers of the body. The central nervous system is inside its bony redoubt, and the most critical life-monitoring mechanisms are further buried in the interior of the brain itself. The most valuable and stable templates of all—the DNA codes—have from the very beginning been stored in the cell nucleus, behind a barrier resistant to any but friendly messengers as long as the cell is intact.

However, if perpetuating what has worked in the past and what is stable in the present were the only values our organisms pursued, we would all still be amoebas, or perhaps we would be nothing at all. We are constantly coming up against novel and unanticipatable objects and events in the environment and in ourselves that we must successfully accommodate. Often in these novel situations the extreme conservative philosophies of "If it's new-fangled, I'm agin it," or "If it ain't broke, don't fix it" are of little use: New information, new structures, and new behaviors are continually being called for in order to explore our world and to keep pace with an evolving ecosystem, our own changing organisms, and their shifting relations. A Model 'T' in good running order may not be "broke," but it nevertheless has distinct operational disadvantages when compared to a well-tuned Ferrari or a Beechcraft.

To this end nature opened up even her most cherished DNA records to a certain amount of exposure and shuffling in order to invite random fluctuations that could lead to positive change. This is the fundamental purpose of sexual reproduction—the recombination of genes inherited from *two different* parent organisms, which serves to produce a much higher ratio of random and possibly useful mutations per generation. This evolutionary leap-frog over the more genetically conservative process of single-cell division was an enormous shift towards *liberalizing* chromosomal development; and this could well be one reason why even today sexual promiscuity tends to be associated with "liberal" leanings, as opposed to a more conservative celibacy or fidelity.

At the core, then, of the liberal strategy is an impulse towards exploration and experimentation—a craving for the unknown and the creative that can be quite as strong as—indeed can sometimes overpower—the "primary" instinct for survival. Once novelty has visited us a few times, and we have successfully integrated it and discovered the unforeseen pleasures and advantages it can generate, we quickly develop an appetite for its unsettling excitement. Anxiety gives way to curiosity, and mere security suddenly appears to be suffocating, suppressing. Once a safe haven has been established, an irrepressible compulsion for *play* exerts itself, and we are off on our other instinctual endeavor: seeing to it that survival is interesting enough, and fun enough, to be worth having.

This element of playfulness is another reason why liberalism is often regarded as a secondary—even a frivolous—value. But this is only because the conservative side of our nature fails to grasp the real significance of "play." Young animals gamboling and tumbling about are not putting off the responsibilities of "real life;" they are preparing for them. They are shuffling their patterns and honing their adaptive reflexes. They are developing free-form strategies for reacting to the unforeseen, strategies that can for the moment *be* free-form *precisely because* they are free of current concerns for survival. In this way, flexibility is introduced into the system, and options for survival under wider and wider circumstances are exponentially enhanced.

This is why the liberal impulse is impatient with precedent; that is merely what worked before. Every cell in a higher organism knows (and perhaps this foreknowledge is precisely what marks it as a "higher" organism) that things are certain to change, that what worked before undoubtedly will not work indefinitely, and that *continued* survival will always depend upon new strategies and adaptations.

"Reliability" takes on a profoundly different meaning in this context, quite the opposite of doggedly reproducing what was done previously. A too-comfortable status quo becomes an irritant to the liberal impulse—a dangerous seduction towards complacency, a fatal reliance upon current conditions. Familiar patterns can themselves be the problem when it comes to creative adaptation, as can authority, hierarchy, or conformity. The silent workings of the conservative unconscious are, to be sure, taken gratefully for granted, but it is the exploratory engagement of the *peripheral* nervous system exposed to the outside world, the kaleidoscopic, voluntary, conscious, sensory stream of experience that delights the liberal instinct. This is the mood and mode of psyche in which change is reveled in for its own sake, not anticipated with foreboding and avoided until a crisis.

Since this kind of experimentation and play appears on the face of it to have little to do with the serious business of survival, it and its products are regarded by those of a conservative cast of mind as superfluous ornamentation, "mere aesthetics." What is forgotten in this stunted characterization is that survival itself is an art, and that survival genuinely worth having is the most aesthetic achievement of all. And when the liberal spirit, captivated by its own speculative enthusiasm and fascination with novelty, casts aspersions upon the inertia of conservatism, forgetting that it is this very inertia which maintains the momentum and trajectory of life, it ultimately does the mind, the body, and society no service.

One of the principle problems in our political debate—and it is escalating to terrifying proportions—is that we tend to characterize these two points of view and the strategies they employ as exclusive and incompatible opposites. Each of us, depending upon our own personal inclinations, identifies all that is good with one point of view and demonizes the other.

This is a war of ideologies, not an exchange of fruitful ideas, and the winner-take-all atmosphere it engenders ensures collective failure regardless of which side wins. Ultimately we are not talking about political parties or administrations that can succeed one another according to the accidents of history. We are talking about polarized life-forces which must operate together with exquisite intimacy and mutual understanding if society, and the individuals of whom it is composed, are to continue to survive.

3

Celebrating Hedonism and Self-Esteem

I have a number of acquaintances from various other parts of the country who regard us Californians as a bunch of flaky touchy-feelies caught up in immature and silly forms of self-indulgence. These folks tend to view hot-tubs as both the height of moral irresponsibility and the nadir of intellectual rigor. I also have an earnest and successful doctor friend who regards bodywork as transitory titillation, pleasant enough while it lasts but certainly without serious therapeutic value.

When Joseph Campbell gave his famous advice on how to succeed in life—"Follow your bliss!"—some reviewers responded as though such an absurd bit of self-serving twaddle was enough to call into question his entire life's work and the scholarly conclusions to which it led him. And when Gloria Steinem, one of the revered warriors of feminism, proposed in her book *The Revolution Within* that a robust sense of self-esteem was one of the crucial ingredients to successful political activism, the cat-calls were all but universal. She might as well have stayed home and baked a batch of cookies. Such obviously self-deluded psychobabble was received in many quarters as nothing short of a betrayal of the troops desperately engaged with the enemy in a battle for women's equality and dignity.

Nature, we are told, is red in tooth and claw. Our nearest evolutionary relatives are chimpanzees—a violently competitive lot. Life comes with no guarantee of joy, or even of moderate

comfort, and bitter struggle against the elements has charac-
terized all of its major developments. The path to genuine
accomplishment is an inherently rigorous one, and by definition rigor is not fun. In order to grow beyond the frivolous
delights of childhood we require discipline, self-sacrifice, a
thorough schooling in hard knocks, tough love, and a good
deal of practice at deferring gratification. We must learn to
"just say no" to any diversion that might deflect our purpose
or weaken our will. Without pain, the saying goes, there can
be no gain, and the value of our accomplishments is the measure of the efforts it takes to produce them.

And yet an important and unique part of our self-declared
political independence from the Old World and of our unique
national identity flies in the face of much of these stern max-
ims: "We hold these truths to be self-evident, that all men are
created equal, that they are endowed by their Creator with
certain unalienable rights, that among these are life, liberty
and the pursuit of happiness." Historically and politically
this last phrase is rather remarkable. No other nation in the
history of the world has included the right to "happiness" in
its written constitution, never mind claiming it as an unalienable right endowed by our Creator. Any number of kings have
assumed *their* right to happiness, but that is about as far as
the concept got. And this particular founding principle is even
more astonishing when we recall that it was conceived and
written by Puritans, whose dour Protestantism would seem to
be worlds away from a vision of a society reveling in even
God-given happiness.

Clearly there is something we have misunderstood about
our philosophical legacy—and something we have misunderstood about ourselves. This singular constitutional phrase
twitches back the mantle covering a tremendous insight into
the potential of human values: Survival itself, our supreme
good without which there are no others, is of questionable value
without at least some measure of happiness to make it worth-
while. And liberty has no real meaning unless every individual

is genuinely free to pursue that measure. So, how are we to understand and identify this "happiness," and how are we to effectively pursue it?

On the face of it, we are a culture that is enthusiastically—even compulsively—wedded to the idea of pleasure. After all, the whole point of Doublemint Gum, and the tens of thousands of other items we can purchase from the shelves so filled with titillations, is to "double your pleasure and double your fun." The consumer ethos, the driving engine of our entire economy, is nothing less than the institutionalization of the pursuit of happiness, which it equates with the pursuit of goods, services, and another largely American invention, fun-filled leisure. For large numbers of people—perhaps even a majority—work has become little more than the odious but necessary means to afford the expenses entailed in free evenings, week-ends, and vacations adequately filled with diversions and delights.

And yet there is a curious retrograde in this headlong pursuit. If, in the midst of this frenzied play, anyone actually states out loud that pleasure is in fact our highest value and chief good, they are accused of "hedonism"—a word that has a distinctly pejorative ring to it. It suggests to us that the speaker is "shallow," or even "perverse." It signifies the exaltation of instant gratification over long-term gains.

It is one of those words that is frequently prefaced by "mere." Worse than that, it smacks of frivolous and addictive preoccupation with values and behaviors that are destructive to our moral fiber. Elevated to a sociological scale, it raises the specter of irresponsible or self-serving pleasures enjoyed at the expense of others. If happiness is consciously enshrined as our highest good, what is to prevent the systematic trashing of all intellectual rigor, civilized norms, or ethical standards in an attempt to remove any perceived restraints from all perceived pleasures?

But are all—or any?—of our hectic pursuits actually headed in the direction of a happiness that is palpable and enduring?

Can we really call our consumer clutter and our busy leisure "pleasures" in the sense that they actually bring genuine satisfaction to genuine psychic and organic desires? The truth is that what is too often missing from such an assessment is an appreciation of the subjective realities and concrete effects of many of the "pleasures" with which we surround ourselves.

Cigarettes, alcohol, and other drugs do in fact deliver pleasant physical and mental effects; but pursued indiscriminately, they will lead to lung disease, liver disease, heart disease, wasted lives and shattered families, none of which are fun. Extensive leisure and conspicuous consumption have long been dreams of most of those who toil, but when our frenetic enjoyment is purchased at the price of feverish competition, mental and physical breakdown, and lethal environmental waste, can we honestly claim to be having the time of our lives? Casual social contact, and above all casual sex, apparently offers all the goodies without any of the encumbrances, but who has failed to notice that these interpersonal pleasures cloy and sour without the necessary inconveniences of commitment, patience, and periodically painful self-development?

In fact, the continued pursuit of most of these perceived pleasures hinges upon the failure to notice and acknowledge their subsequent effects either upon ourselves or upon others. What our current hedonism presently suffers from is not a surfeit of pleasure, but rather a superficial sense of what might constitute a genuine pleasure, a cerebral dislocation of our pleasures from our actual senses, from the biological foundations that ultimately deliver to us all punishment and all reward.

The problem is not that pleasure per se is merely fleeting, unreliable, morally or physically destructive. The problem is that we have surrounded ourselves with so many fleeting, unreliable, and destructive pleasures. This is why Wilhelm Reich, a hedonist in the most respectable sense of the term, was so widely and violently misunderstood, and why his cry to awaken our basically sensual nature was regarded by so many as demonically misguided. "I was accused," he wrote in *The Function of the Orgasm,* "of being a utopian, of wanting to eliminate unpleasure from the world and safeguard pleasure only....*Pleasure and joy of life are inconceivable without struggle, painful experiences, and unpleasurable self-confrontations.*"

There is another related word from the same Greek root that might help us back towards a biological basis for discerning pleasure and its psychological and physiological significance. When psychologists want to characterize a positive emotional reaction to something that an animal associates with positive survival value, they call that reaction "hedonic". This verbal modification skirts all the negative self-indulgent connotations, and simply speaks directly to the feeling tone that is appropriately aroused when we encounter something useful, live-preserving or life-enhancing, both enjoyable and adaptive.

We are drawn forward towards further exploration of things and events that have positive survival value, and we instinctively withdraw to avoid those things and events which do not. This is the sense in which, "It is natural," as the Maharishi Mahesh Yogi has said, "for the mind to move towards the fields of greater happiness." He was referring neither to cheap thrills nor to esoteric spiritual accomplishments, but rather to the normal state of emotional and behavioral responses as a healthy and successful organism goes about its daily business of living and learning.

These positive inclinations and negative repulsions have a constant, a fundamental, and a pervasive impact upon the development of the organism. They define the parameters of an appropriate niche, and they define our relationship to everything within it. And more than that, they define our relationship to our own psychology and physiology. Hans Selye exhaustively documented the devastating pathological ramifications of stressful unpleasure on organisms, and Herbert

Benson (*The Relaxation Response*) has carefully documented the complementary positive influences of meditation, relaxation, and pleasurable affect. The unequivocal conclusion is that both pleasure and unpleasure reach deeply into the biochemistry and developmental viability of all organisms.

One of the primary reactions to unpleasure—and one that almost all modalities of bodywork address directly in one way or another—is that it raises muscle tonus, the process of "armoring" that Reich researched and described. This can happen locally around specific physical discomforts, segmentally in psychologically associated areas, or system-wide in response to a more general threat. If either the discomfort persists or the response becomes habituated, then a long line of organic dominoes begins to tumble. These accumulating conditions establish an internal scenario for disease and dysfunction that can be both subtle in detail and devastating in collective impact, and which requires no germs or genes to set it in motion.

Now this is exactly where sensory "pleasuring" derives its survival value: It is one of nature's key antidotes to these pernicious developments, and this is why evolution has so highly developed our sensual capacities for pleasure in the first place. The mind *attends* to pleasure, is inclined towards it, opens its listening channels in order to amplify it, strives to accommodate and sustain it. It is *hedonic*. And through these expanded portals of positive affect come streaming clearer, more complete, and more detailed sensory *information*—without which the finest brain cannot successfully direct internal biological traffic or external behavior.

Any organism that can surrender its defensive armoring, attend to genuine biological (as opposed to merely socially acculturated) pleasure, and integrate the information that comes along with it has the capacity to self-regulate towards a continually developing optimal. With this capacity comes the sense of feeling safe and at home within one's own skin, which is the concrete foundation of *self-esteem*.

And this is exactly where bodywork enters as a significant survival strategy for the painful situations in which we find ourselves. The confusions about sensory pleasure that we have inherited have diminished and garbled this flow of self-regulatory information immeasurably and robbed us of a clear self-image and the ability to act internally on our own behalf. This is the real meaning of *impotence*—not simply the incapacity for sexual gratification, but the tortuous incapacity for a wide range of hedonic, self-regulatory behaviors. There is some truth to the view of nature as "red in tooth and claw," but advancing this metaphor for the food chain to the status of the primary driving force of evolution—"survival of the fittest"—is a great conceptual mistake. There is vastly more watchful and peaceful cooperation and mutual respect of boundaries in nature than ruthless competition. And, of course, the other equally important pressure that perpetuators the continuation of new genetic traits and more successful adaptation is the pressure to reproduce—"survival of those that get off the most."

Now, as professional bodyworkers we are rightly concerned with the association of sex and massage, but there is in fact an important connection here that we need not—indeed should not—eschew: Eros in its widest and most significant dimensions means the hedonic pleasure associated with the surrender to *all* of the pleasure-giving physical and mental processes that genuinely contribute to the vitality of our internal life and contribute to our survival as individuals and as a species.

Incidentally, this is why emotional and sexual abuse are so damaging. They deeply confuse pleasure-giving touch and nurturing human contact with unwanted intrusion, and by conditioning us to avoid intimate contacts of all kinds and at all costs this intrusion compels us to starve ourselves of the necessary ingredients for our survival. Bodywork is often a dramatic solution to these crippling confusions and reactions, because it gives an individual a safe place and a safe time in which to work out meaningful distinctions that have been hopelessly scrambled.

This association with the larger dimensions of Eros and self-gratification does not in any way blur the line between the sensory pleasures of bodywork and those of sexuality. On the contrary, it emphasizes the differences emphatically, and creates a definite and reliable boundary between the two. It is, in fact, *violation* of that boundary that blurs the distinctions, introducing the self-destructive confusions between sex and all *other* forms of self-loving, comfort-giving, information-laden sensory pleasures.

Sorting out these distinctions and rediscovering these capacities are precisely what all this massage and hot-tub and group therapy business is all about, and if it looks silly and self-indulgent from the point of view that a good deal of the country calls "traditional," then that is exactly where the debate needs to be taken up. The tradition from which they speak is exactly the one that we are all up against, and I simply can't see that it has served us particularly well.

I earnestly believe that the early Americans were right—happiness, and the pleasure that engenders it, are unalienable rights, simply because they are necessary conditions for healthy development and survival. I cannot see how you can prepare anyone for "reality" by denying them pleasure, cutting them off from their own sensory information, and injuring their self-esteem. B.F. Skinner did get that one thing right: Punishment is a very poor teaching tool. Heightening positive expectation with hedonic rewards is vastly more effective.

This is what President Clinton was alluding to when he declared in a State of the Union Address that "we must give our children something to say 'yes' to." What we are witnessing in the state of our social union is that the kind of mutual tolerance and respect necessary to democracy is devilishly difficult to achieve among individuals who have not been taught to both value the inherent pleasures of nurturing human contact and to successfully regulate their own health and comfort.

So embrace these yeasty hedonic pleasures and plunge happily and without reservation into the delights of nurture waiting in your treatment room, and savor the new measure of self-esteem it brings both you and your clients at the end of your day. As Dr. Milton Trager has said, "Every shimmer of the tissue is sending a message to the unconscious mind in the form of a positive feeling experience. It is the accumulation of these positive patterns that can offset the negative patterns to the point where the positive can take over." This is not temporary titillation. It is the active engagement of hedonic responses that have been faithful guidelines for millennia of survival and evolution, and that are the true foundations of pleasure, health, and biologically sound happiness.

4

Touch the Children

On the morning of March 10th 1994, Neil Shumate, a kindergarten teacher in Pleasanton, California, was sitting in the Santa Rita Jail in lieu of $100,000 bond. Mr. Shumate was charged with seven counts of lewd and lascivious conduct—"fondling"—with five of his pupils, three girls and two boys all aged five and six.

According to the Pleasanton police chief, several of the charges involved "skin-on-skin" contact. That all of the alleged abuses occurred in the presence of other children, and in most instances in a classroom with a wide open door, was never denied by the authorities. At his arraignment, the courtroom was packed with Mr. Shumate's sympathizers. "I would trust Mr. Shumate with my life," said a female neighbor of 22 years, "and more importantly, the lives and well-being of my own children." The mother of one of the girls in Shumate's class expressed adamant skepticism at the charges; others observed that he was a "hugger," and that his tendency to be physically affectionate—with adults as well as children—might have been misinterpreted. Despite these supportive testimonies and despite the lack of any evidence whatever that injury occurred to any child, Mr. Shumate was sentenced to six years in prison.

There is a disturbing vagueness and innuendo in these reports that may not bode well for the good name of any teacher, or even for the real well-being of their students, whether or not the absence of lascivious intent can be successfully demonstrated in this specific instance. Can we—either as adults *or* children—truly not tell the difference between affectionate physical contact with a variety of adults—which every child requires for healthy development—and unwanted sexual advances on the helpless, which is inevitably damaging?

Is "skin-on-skin" contact an automatic barrier in public institutions for children, across which lie pathology and criminality? Isn't it important *which* skin exactly is involved, and the manner in which it is touched? What is the effect upon children of the message that adult affection is inherently dangerous? Are affection and perversion so closely allied in people's minds that reliable distinctions can no longer be made between "huggers, muggers, and buggers"?

Perhaps Mr. Shumate is guilty and damned. On the other hand, his dilemma may expose confusions surrounding some primary issues of child care that have the potential to be every bit as damaging as anything he is suspected of having done. Coping with those confusions matters very much, not only to the possibly innocent Mr. Shumate but also to his definitely innocent students. Discouraging or prohibiting affectionate touch between them merely attempts to avoid one possible pathology by systematically enforcing another.

Child abuse is certainly horrific, and certainly has been far more common than previous generations had assumed or admitted. Not only is it painful for the child at the time, but the inevitable feelings of helplessness, humiliation, fear, guilt, and rage persist throughout a lifetime. The work and writing of Alice Miller (*Drama of the Gifted Child, For Your Own Good, Thou Shalt Not Be Aware*) document these effects and their relentless conclusions with frightening insight: Abuse powerfully tends to perpetuate abuse, as the traumatized child's compulsion for personal vengeance grows to overwhelming adult proportions and finds its outlets in the punishment of his or her own children, domestic violence, racial and gender hatreds, murders and assaults, or the fiercer forms of nationalism, and war.

And there is no question that these horrors of physical abuse are typically amplified even further by specifically *sexual* abuse, which adds altogether new dimensions to the pain, humiliation, and sense of betrayal. Furthermore, it is quite possible that *ostensibly* affectionate sexual abuses—those that are perpetrated by familiar and "loving" adults whose "fondling" would normally be pleasurable—are among the very worst sort, precisely because they play so cynically upon the innocent child's needs and trust as well as upon its weakness. One of life's most insistent biological urges, and one of life's chief physical pleasures becomes tainted and twisted up in the brutal tangle of pain, denial, and compensatory behaviors.

These kinds of injuries are undoubtedly among the root causes of the perennial hidden wars that toil on day and night even as nations are at peace—the wars between adult and child, between genders, between the strong and the weak on all fronts, and between the conflicted fragments of a broken psyche. And when all has been said and done, it is likely that *these* wars account for more casualties and human loss than the official, international or civil ones.

But—and I believe this caveat is an enormously important one—we *do not* therefore avoid damaged children by simply outlawing affectionate contact by adults or by erecting barriers around any and all "skin-on-skin" encounters in order to somehow guarantee the prevention of lascivious intent and criminal abuse. Yes, we absolutely owe these children the assurance of safe and nurturing conditions in which to grow, and to this end they must be protected against the evils of molestation. But for exactly the same reason we must not isolate them from the touch—lots of touch and genuinely affectionate touch—of the adults that are supervising their development. There can be no argument that unhealthy intrusion can be, usually is, a catastrophe for a child; what is perhaps less well understood is that physical abandonment and the lack of nurturing touch can be equally damaging. Indeed, when carried to extremes this deficit is lethal.

Nor is this merely a matter of providing emotional warmth. What is at stake here is a wide variety of physical, mental, and social developments that strike to the very heart of a growing individual's survival and viability, let alone his or her happiness. The varying degrees of devastation resulting from touch deprivation have been repeatedly documented in hundreds of clinical studies involving many kinds of mammals including humans. The data is unequivocal, and absolutely cannot be ignored if we are truly interested in providing an environment for our children and our society that is both "safe" and genuinely "nurturing."

In 1915 two independent American researchers, James Knox, Jr. and Henry Dwight Chapin, published studies documenting that almost 99% of the children delivered to orphanages in this country in their first year of life died before twelve months of age of a mysterious disease called *merasmus*, "wasting away." Follow-up investigations of these ghastly numbers revealed that the single most important factor was the chronic under staffing of the orphanages; there was simply not enough help to give physical attention to the infants beyond the brief contacts during feeding and changing. The solution, immediately successful, was to fund the institutions to hire additional staff so that each infant could be affectionately "fondled" during their day. Thus modern scientific methodology demonstrated what husbandmen and zookeepers had long known: No newborn can survive without enough tactile stimulation.

In 1920 Frederick S. Hammett was studying the functions of the thyroid and parathyroid glands in rats by removing them and examining the causes of subsequent death. Curiously skewed statistical results in different groups of rats in the laboratory led him to make inquiries among his team members, who turned out to be giving the rats under their supervision very different sorts of treatment both before and after the surgeries. One group was ignored except for feeding and cage-cleaning, while another was "fondled" frequently by their handler. All the rats, of course, eventually died. But 79% of the ignored rats died within 24 hours of their surgery, while only 13% of the fondled rats died in the same time period.

Further observation of human beings in this context led to the recognition of "deprivation dwarfism," a condition of physical deformation and mental retardation that mimics the effects of severe malnutrition: stunted size, misshapen skeleton, organ dysfunction, autism, poor learning abilities, and so on. In fact, its effects are so consistently destructive that some researchers now feel that the diminishment of stimulation in weakened, malnourished children may itself account for a good deal of their developmental symptoms. It begins to appear as though there are few stresses as damaging as that of being unfondled, untouched.

A famous series of experiments with rhesus monkeys by Harry Harlow in the 1950's drove this conclusion even further home. Baby monkeys were given various combinations of two surrogate mothers—one of cold wire with a nursing bottle attached, one of soft, warm terry cloth with no milk supply. Given a choice, *all* of the subjects preferred spending time with the soft, milkless "mother," by a ratio of about fifteen hours a day to one. In threatening situations, they chose to huddle about the soft, warm one. Those raised exclusively with the wire/milk surrogate were severely underdeveloped physically and mentally, and severely disturbed emotionally. Harlow had expected something like this to emerge from his data, but he was astonished at the enormity of the craving for and biological importance of creature-comfort compared to feeding time. "Certainly," he concluded, "man cannot live by milk alone." Touch is food. Vital food.

Many follow-up studies have documented the details of what exactly goes wrong with organisms that are not touched enough: They have smaller brain-weights, due both to smaller cell bodies and to less myelin insulating sheaths around axons; specifically, they have thinner cerebral cortexes. Their nerve cells also evidence lower metabolic rates. Synaptic junctions tend to be as much as 50% smaller. They grow more slowly, have less developed skeletal muscular systems, inferior coordination, depressed immunological resistance, less pronounced pituitary/adrenal activity, later puberties, and are less successful breeders and nursers. They are much more emotionally distressed. They are less lively, less curious, less active problem solvers, less willing to explore new environments, and advance more slowly in all forms of conditioned learning exercises.

How can all these things be accounted for? "The answer is quite simple," says Ashley Montagu in his seminal book *Touching: The Human Significance of the Skin*. "Tactile stimulation appears to be a fundamentally necessary experience for the healthy behavioral development of the individual....The raw sensation of touch as stimulus is vitally necessary for the physical survival of the organism. In that sense it may be postulated that the need for tactile stimulation must be added to the repertoire of basic needs in all vertebrates...."

These findings have some interesting implications for many of the social problems and health problems we currently observe in our culture. Much of what passes for learning disabilities or poor school systems may to a significant degree be the result of these kinds of depressed physical and mental performances. Health care is also less effective in a population suffering invisibly from such developmental deficits. Many juvenile delinquents, who are getting more and more violently aggressive, are quite possibly engaged in a desperate search for some form, any form, of attention and stimulation: Deep within their physical organism they carry the knowledge that physical abuse is preferable to isolation in an uncaring world. Here may also be some insight into the reasons why impoverished and under-educated young girls would tolerate, or even welcome, the sexual attentions of older males, and why they might yearn in some way for the measure of additional care often received during pregnancy and for the company of an infant they cannot possibly support.

Indeed, these are only some of the more glaring examples we might point to. There are undoubtedly vast gray areas of marginal dysfunctions occurring in large segments of a population that distrusts or devalues touch. This silent, invisible, germless pathology surely scatters many partial victims in its wake, victims with nothing physiologically concrete to diagnose, but whose weakened and aggravated conditions interferes with their lives sufficiently to erode their work performances, disrupt their domestic stability, limit their learning capacities, and help to dispose them towards apathy, drugs, or crime.

Clearly, then, abusive touch and *no* touch are both enormously devastating, potentially lethal, and permanently scarring, each in their own ways. We cannot protect our children by sliding them from the frying pan of abuse into the fire of sensory abandonment. These necessary distinctions force us to actively work out the gross and subtle differences between *damaging* and *nourishing* touch. The biological and psychological issues that hang in the balance cannot be papered over by simplistic regulations and child-rearing practices based on nothing more than avoidance. Moral and educational rules and values that are divorced from the actual biological needs of the child can never in the end be anything other than pernicious, no matter what they are seeking to prove or prevent. They simply cannot be enforced if physical and mental health is the goal, if maximum vitality and optimal development are genuinely desired ends.

Appropriate, affectionate, nourishing touch is one of the main missing ingredients in our social fabric. The very fact that modalities of health care which consciously utilize it are referred to as "alternatives" speaks worlds. This is not simply sad; this is disastrous. It is possible, in fact, to view deliberate *non-touching* as a form of abuse, perpetuated compulsively by those who were not touched as growing children who now are avenging themselves for the painful and damaging deprivations they suffered. This is why as a society we are earnestly in need of "touch professionals," individuals whose life-experience and training have equipped them with both the touching skills and the ethical perspectives that can help sort out the confusions and begin to perpetuate more positive contacts.

"Fondling," for instance, is an extremely ambiguous word. It can, and is used to, mean everything from petting rats in the laboratory to bouncing baby on mother's knee to molesting kindergartners. What could have been crucial for the case of Mr. Shumate was the possibility of a jury of his peers that could genuinely understand and appreciate these ambiguities and distinctions. The truth is, of course, that it is statistically likely that they themselves had been touch-deprived to one degree or another, and so....

Overt behavior can and does define *some* of the parameters. There are after all obvious pieces of children's skin that should not under any circumstances be touched by adults in whose care they are placed. "Lewd" and "lascivious" are not nearly as ambiguous as "fondling." *Intent* is clearly a major issue; this is to a degree subjective, but subjective impressions that carry this kind of weight are just as capable of clear definition and recognition as any observable behavior. After all, the entire issue of adult sexual harassment revolves around the ability and responsibility to acknowledge when a tacit subjective barrier has been crossed.

As it happens, the surest way to be able to tell the difference between touch that violates and touch that nourishes is to receive a great deal of the latter at all stages of life. Then any contact with the former is glaringly obvious and unwelcome. Touch professionals working with adults can facilitate the *recovery* of those who were either abused or deprived. But reaching the children in time with the kind and amount of contact they require to build strong bodies and minds, firm boundaries, and healthy social relations is the only thing that will prevent the need for continual rehabilitation and recovery in every new generation.

Human touch, with its pleasures and demonstrable physical and mental benefits is part of the birthright of every child born, and the bodywork profession will not be finished with the "mainstreaming" of its work until its nurturing influence is standard fare in the grade school, the preschool, and the nursery.

5

Somatic Education and Evolution

Individuals develop. Species evolve. Sometimes for the better, sometimes for the worse. A strong case can readily be made for the positive role of bodywork in the former. A broad consensus of scientific opinion would insist that bodywork does not, cannot, play any role at all in the latter. It is maintained as a fundamental principle of evolution that the complex processes of genetic recombination and random mutation are untouched either by the environment or by individual experience.

But can the evolutionary future of creatures as complicated and as richly endowed with open-ended options as human beings really have nothing whatever to do with how they learn, what they learn, and how they learn to behave? However we answer this, the specific biochemical mechanisms of chromosomal mutation clearly consititute only one of the forces driving us whither. Mutations must *endure* in order to become significant, and this part of the process raises altogether different questions.

Other animals *have* a body, and *have* a particular place in a particular niche; but to a large degree humans must *develop* active, conscious, and continually changing relationships with these things. The pressures of natural selection and survival have escalated our complexity to the level that we now have an extraordinary range of choices available to us in these relationships—choices so broad as to make each individual something of a species unto him- or herself. In the same way that cats act like cats and dogs act like dogs, humans can cultivate themselves to act like typists, artists, athletes, dancers, couch potatoes, scholars, doctors, murderers, rapists, teachers, truck drivers...the list is endless. And each of these options involves distinctive physical and mental patterning and creative developments of our anatomy that differentiate our personal structure, chemistry, and function as effectively as many examples of actual mutation.

But—and this is the principle challenge to us both as individuals and as a species—infinite choices do not come without the ability to make infinite mistakes, small and large. Some of those choices have made us the most successful species on the planet. And some will perhaps confront us with social and political developments as threatening as anything that confronted the dinosaurs.

Evolutionary sophistication, in short, has irretrievably forced humans to be *clever* in order to use our heritage for survival. Our somatic education cannot be left to the unconscious unfolding of instincts and reflexes. To the degree to which this is true, the rich potentials of our sophisticated biological inheritance have *necessitate* bodywork, somatic education—some kind of conscious, exploratory, and systematic way of teaching ourselves and our offspring how to successfully use, and not abuse, the potent range of physical and mental possibilities contained within us.

It is not, to be sure, that bodywork directly alters genes. It is rather that the genetic developments that we represent now absolutely require somatic education in order to be successfully *organized*, both for individuals to survive and for there to be a species that can continue to evolve. Somatic education of one kind or another is for us an obligatory part of our collective development, as much a part of our fate as any chromosome. And this is not the sort of fact that can be rendered inoperative by neglect.

At this point it is all but impossible for us to imagine the impact of Darwin's ideas upon the culture of his place and time. His rigorous biological departure from traditional points of view left whole roomful of intellectual and spiritual furniture turned upside down. And I suspect that he would have been no less disruptive had he been able to anticipate the profusion of insights and conundrums that continue to be generated by the far-reaching debate he launched. We are still reeling with the riddles and consequences of our origins, the shape of our history, and the potential directions of our destiny that are implied by the theory of natural selection and a rigorous biological examination of human development.

Nor, at this point, can we simply turn our backs upon the difficult questions that are raised by this examination. Humanity has always been obliged to search for better ways of behaving, and in the midst of the dilemmas created by our modern industrial and political society, that search has become ever more desperate. Mankind may cling to a past or aspire to a future, but as Jung observed in *An Answer to Job*, "he can make no progress with himself unless he becomes very much better acquainted with his own nature." That nature is biological, and for better or worse biology evolves. How it does so and where it is going matters.

On the one hand, Darwin thrust us into the midst of the activities of the planet and the cosmos with a physical, material intimacy quite different from that of then-prevailing biological theories or religious visions: We are literally woven from the same fabric as the world, emergent from the same fundamental properties and laws that characterize all matter and all forms of life. We are caught up by and actively engaged in a vast process of becoming, a process that embraces the whole universe, a process that ties our breath to the winds, our blood to the tides, our heartbeat to time, and our vitality to the prolific creativity of Nature.

On the other hand, this intimate association with the rest of the natural world leads to some chilling—not to say damning—

observations and associations: Nature is value-neutral and frighteningly impersonal. Many must die so that others may live. A great deal of the evolutionary process is experimental, and errors are mercilessly erased by virtue of their own dysfunction. There is a relentless competition for resources in any niche, for the privilege of mating, and for the survival of offspring. Significant changes in morphology and behavior come about only through "mutation," a mindlessly random slot machine of chromosomal combinations. Rather than conjoining the processes of human development with the laws that govern the rest of the cosmos, evolutionary theory in the minds of many render us unto forces and processes that are defined as basically mechanistic and biochemical, intelligible but unintelligent, inhuman, uncaring, unfolding how they will, an infuriatingly destabilized mix of luck and strict determinism in which statistical odds take the place of divine decree or conscious intent.

One of the few constants in this flux, the phrase that has come to typify the broad consequences of Darwin's theories, is "the survival of the fittest." This has been generally taken to mean the supremacy of brute strength, competitive reproduction or superior defense. Furthermore, these survival traits had to come about by means of chance reshuffling of genetic materials at conception, not by intent on the part of the individual or design on the part of some "Creator." The influences of consciousness, learning, and culture are categorically eliminated from the factors generating the genetic mutations and lasting evolution developments of any species. Therefore, for many scientists and philosophers thought and sensibility and experience can have nothing to do with evolutionary progress in the biological realm; they are mere spin-offs, side effects, epiphenomena that may be interesting from a psychological point of view but which are without significance in the evolutionary scheme of things. Indeed, the intellectual and emotional force of this account of things has become so powerful that it has quite overwhelmed an obvious observation:

In a vast number of both general and individual cases, it is "the survival of the *cleverest*," or "the survival of the most successfully cooperative" that really counts.

Lamarck, a contemporary of Darwin, championed a different version of evolutionary theory that sought to include individual experience and intent in the mechanisms of mutation. He held that characteristics acquired in the course of the parents' lives could be transferred genetically to their offspring—that the environment and learning itself could alter the encoding of DNA. This has turned out to be wrong—there appears to be no mechanism whereby life experience can *alter the structure* of the genes—and Lamarck's defeat in the debate was widely considered to be the death-knell of any link between intelligence or intent and evolutionary change. Smarter creatures may well fare better *individually*, but there is no genetic mechanism for transferring this fortuitous advantage on to their offspring.

Yet is it really necessary to concede that intelligence, and the novel forms of behavior that it can develop, count for nothing in the grand scheme of things, that consciousness is a mere curiosity with no net effect? No. What is true is that Darwinian selection and Lamarckian transference are not mutually exclusive, one right and the other simply wrong. They are different mechanisms operating in different spheres of influence, often—and most spectacularly in the case of human beings—dramatically reinforcing one another.

Natural selection may for instance not merely produce a closer and closer match of creature characteristics to the demands of a particular niche. It may, through random mutations, confer new *capacities for learning* behaviors that lead to superior adaptability and survival. Individuals who inherit such capacities, and who *succeed in learning to utilize them appropriately*, will naturally have higher survival rates and a correspondingly higher chance of mating and passing their mutations on as a permanent feature of their gene pool. Insofar as acquired experience can definitely have survival value, the genetic *capacity* for acquiring and applying experience can and does play a significant and sometimes decisive role in species development. Intelligence—and muddleheadedness—count.

In other words, as Gregory Bateson observed in *Mind and Nature: A Necessary Unity*, "The *potentiality* for somatic change becomes the object of selection."

Now our brains are, after all, a significant part of our functional anatomy, the part that directs the functions of all the rest. It follows then that changes in brain morphology can have far greater impact on behavior and adaptability, "somatic change," than any other kind—say, a new kind of claw, or hue of plumage, or digestive abilities, or mating patterns. Indeed, in the estimation of Gerald Edelman, a contemporary neurologist and Nobel laureate, "The brain is the most variable of all complex systems" during the course of evolution, and after a critical threshold of complexity is reached its further development expands rapidly and enormously the capacities for exploration, perception, learning, memory, language, adaptability, and somatic change.

Our brains, bodies, posture, and locomotion patterns have in fact become so complex and variable in their specific interactions that they have become part of the world which requires exploration, categorization, and organization. And how we organize them changes how they explore, perceive, and learn novel ways to use themselves. As Edelman states it,

"Out of the increase in complexity of evolutionary systems, more sophisticated somatic selection systems emerged. With the further increase in the complexity of somatic systems and their linkage to so many aspects of the phenotype, richly linked categorization and novel responses emerged. And finally, out of the interaction of individuals in species capable of social transmission, informational systems emerged. *At this level of transcendence, Larmarckian characteristics are superimposed upon a fundamental Darwinian base.* The degree of complexity of such transmission systems is apparently endless: the number of sentences in a language is infinite.... From so complex an emergence, no obvious end can be visualized."

This is to say that human consciousness is a stupendous wild card in evolution's game of chance. Nature's lottery has cast up in us a new kind of number, one which transcends both the random and the deterministic qualities of its precursors. A mode of evolving behavior has been created in us that dramatically sidesteps the slowly accumulative process of chromosomal mutation and natural selection. Evolution can and did proceed nicely before the emergence of analytical intelligence, language, memory, learning, and the transference of knowledge and skills. But once these elements enter the formula, the nature, scope, and timetable of somatic change and the possibilities for new survival strategies are altered drastically.

At this stage of social development, then, what I *teach* my child is as important as the genetic codes his mother and I bequeath to him. Indeed, even more so, in the sense that without the benefit of my experience he will not learn the intricacies of his biological inheritance quickly enough to organize his capacities for survival. And if I, along with other members of his tribe, do not instill in him the basic functional principles of his organism's capacities, he will not be able to successfully adapt them to the continually shifting demands he is certain to encounter.

"So it seems," says Charlotte Selver, "that the only real significance in using our potentials lies in the *quality with which we use them.*" And the ways in which we can use them can be endlessly creative, repetitive and muddled, or terminally counterproductive. Raw capacity itself is as sublimely neutral as Shiva on this issue. "This means," continues Selver, "that superimposed education will have to be laid aside, if we are to return to those values which nature has given us. We have to rediscover them. We have to learn anew—like children—to use our biological potentials. In this process the wisdom inherent in our own body can guide us."

Now of course this is exactly where somatic education can, does, *must* enter the picture. We have been issued a manual for the operation of our unit: The vast storage of information and possibilities that is our body itself. All that is necessary is to learn to read it, and all that is necessary for that is to actively engage in the language of movement and sensory awareness, the language of touch. In this endeavor I cannot teach my child anything I have not honestly and actively learned myself, and I cannot pass it on without engaging his intentional activity as well. Only when we touch and respond, and only when we learn about ourselves and one another through that touch, only then is there a teaching and a learning of the body's wisdom, a genuinely functional addition to the acquired repertoire of the species.

Again Bateson: "Growth and differentiation must be controlled by communication. The shapes of animals and plants are transforms of messages. Language is itself a form of communication. The structure of the input must somehow be reflected as structure in the output. Anatomy *must* contain an analog of grammar because all anatomy is a transform of message material, which must be contextually shaped. And finally, *contextual shaping* is only another term for *grammar*." It has *always* been about the successful organization of information.

From the Darwinian emerged the Lamarckian, and from the Lamarckian the new significance of human consciousness as an active force in evolution. Quite possibly the mushrooming of the neocortex from primate to Homo Sapiens was the biggest gamble in all of biological evolution. What is increasingly apparent is that the potent and interactive forces which it imposes upon our physical being can either reorganize ourselves and our world in astonishing new ways or drive us with our new and uncontrolled powers towards a maelstrom of oblivion. In this uncertain voyage, from which we cannot now pull back, our physical and mental contact with the tissue of our lives constitutes our only hand on the tiller. Mute nature began the journey. Biology improved the vessel. Consciousness filled it with treasures. Only somatic education can successfully steer it towards a safe and happy port.

6

The Voices of Angels

Take your well-disciplined strengths and stretch them between two opposing poles. Because inside human beings is where God learns.

RAINER MARIA RILKE *(trans. Robert Bly)*

If the spate of related books, tapes, articles, and seminars is a true indication, a lot of angels are talking to a lot of folks these days. Perhaps not as vociferously as in ages past, when every sigh of the breeze and every clap of thunder was the voice of a deity, but noticeably more than in recent history. And why not? After all, it was Angel Raphael who visited Adam and Eve in the garden, and explained to them the names, the rules and the layout. And what with recent events, it certainly appears as though we could use some advice from a higher order of intelligence.

But to what degree do we have the leisure—or the reliable access—to depend upon the angels? Or, on the other hand, given the tangle we are in, do we have a real choice? Should I take personal responsibility for discovering the truth and setting things right, or will I and the world be better served by fervently waiting for the revelations of the angels and their divinely efficacious interventions?

A major theme of many alternative therapies that are emerging contemporaneously with the new wave of angels—bodywork very much included—is the development of self-awareness and self-responsibility. We have been too long in the thrall of the "experts," both secular and divine, and this has dulled our sensitivities, obscured our choices, atrophied our will to act on our own behalf. We must reengage our subjective awareness and learn to rely much more on what our bodies tell us directly about our problems and what to do about them. My sensorium is an exquisitely acute instrument for perceiving reality, and my physiological functions are highly developed to successfully react to that reality. All that is necessary is that I undertake to learn how to use them properly; our own resources are very often our best defense against ignorance, accidents, and deceit. And touch and movement are among the best contexts for this learning to take place.

And yet, is it truly wise to forsake the wisdom, the consolation, and the strength of the angels in this quest for more complete self-responsibility?

A self-reliance that is too complete may cut me off from powers that sustain me and can improve me. Pride for all that I am is only a misstep away from hubris for what I merely pretend to be, and crossing this line, as the Greeks knew, invites tragedy with all its sufferings. Best to keep an ear out for the divine whispers of more reliable guides on the brink of this precipice.

True humility—readiness to admit what we are not, willingness to learn anything from anyone who knows more—is a good thing; and an ability to learn from angels is a very good thing indeed. But feeling small, and ignorant, and helpless—self-abnegation, even fervently prayerful self-abnegation—is very different. This is false humility, which we adopt for a variety of reasons, none of which have anything to do with an accurate assessment either of our personal powers or of our limitations in the broader context. We do it because we shy away from the attention our strengths might attract. Or we do it because the angels frighten us, and we don't really want to hear what they have to say anyway. We do it to avoid

the conflict and discomfort that exercising our power sometimes entails. We do it to deny that there is anything we *could*
do about the situation, thereby relieving ourselves of the obli-
gation to do it. And we do it in order to side-step the guilt and
shame we might feel if we accepted our active role in our situation in the first place.

So while we create tyranny and tragedy when we pretend
to omnipotence, we scarcely do better when we pretend to
impotence, and give away our power. Tyrants, after all, would
have short careers if a sufficient number of people did not
surrender their better judgment. One of the challenges before
us, and one which somatic education can certainly enhance,
is the conscious recognition of the rather astonishing thing
each of us actually is, and just how penetrating that "better
judgment" can be.

From the Big Bang burst forth an expanding, self-regulating chaos, congealing into countless worlds. Developments in
our corner of the cosmos produced the Blue Planet, which in
turn produced life, eventually evolving humanity and the human brain. We are the actively evolving growth tips of a vast
tree, and we are the most complex and unpredictable creatures we have yet discovered.

Out in space, the direction we typically point to Heaven,
forces are lifeless, turbulent and extreme, dispersed over enormous reaches of space and time. We are the current result of
ages of condensation, organization, stabilization, and the
emergence of unprecedented combinations of elements and
processes. This life force required both extraordinary circumstances to develop and an awesome tenacity for survival once
it was generated. And as it developed, it—we—added something remarkable to the picture: Consciousness. We are the
cosmos looking at itself in a state of self-reflective awareness.

Looking out at the immensity, it is all but impossible to not
feel infinitesimal, inconsequential. But dimension is only one
way to measure size and potency. Black holes are not all that
big either, relatively speaking. And all of the matter and energy

in the Universe, when it was tightly packed into the primordial ball before the Big Bang, was by some physicists' calculations smaller in circumference than the Earth. What now looks so huge is mostly nothing.

On the other hand, that small clot of nerves in my cranium, that narrow fraction of my body's size and weight, is the most complicated object of which we are aware. Super-computers are getting more super every day; but if I connected together all of the computers presently in existence, their collective capacity would not even approach the level of information processing that is going on in the brain of a two-year old learning to walk or talk. We are truly cosmic, not on the scale of our size, but on the scale of our interconnectedness. Given the number of neurons in your nervous system (10 billion, more or less), and the number of synaptic connections that join them together (up to 15,000 on a single motor neuron), and the possibly 300 neuropeptides that can alter the specific function of every neuron, there are more different activity patterns possible within your central nervous system than there are atoms in the known universe.

And it is towards this increased complexity of brain morphology and function that evolution has been exerting its pressures. We have emerged as a spectacularly—even dangerously—successful species not because we are bigger or stronger or more armed and armored or better camouflaged or more poisonous, but because we are more clever. Because we can work out more complicated and flexible strategies, and adapt to new ones when the necessity arises. Because we can learn, and remember, and record memories and pass on learning to others. Because we are an inexhaustible and open-ended potential of choices, not a finite repertoire of finely honed inherited reflexes ideally suited to a particular set of circumstances.

And it is this neuronal synergy, this emergence of self-reflective awareness, accumulative experience, and informed choice that has created for us a slim but crucial measure of *controlled freedom* (not merely random spontaneity with unpredictable results)——a precious sliver of divine creativity that does not appear to be possessed, at least in anything like the same degree, by atoms or molecules or proteins or any animals with significantly simpler brains.

Because we are born unfinished and will be unfinished until we die; because our brain morphology generates a capacity to learn rather than defines stereotyped responses; because we possess the power of choice —in short, because our thoughts and feelings and experiences and voluntary behaviors impact our developing bodies in many powerful ways— we continually participate, whether we notice or not, in the creation of ourselves. It is, after all, a commonplace among bodyworkers to observe that our flesh is the written record of our lives, faithful in every last detail. We are all to a large degree self-made; we are both the hand and the clay.

Hence the critical importance of sensory awareness, of sustained engagement with and observation of the physical tendencies at work within ourselves, and the conscious cultivation of habits and strategies that will lead us towards strength and health rather than towards dysfunction, that will enact our desires rather than act out our compulsions. Hence the importance of bodywork, and its practical and applicable lessons in sensory awareness and behavior modification.

These kinds of responsibilities to our personal being may not be obvious at the outset, but they can be readily recognized and owned with a little knowledgeable guidance. What can be considerably more difficult to grasp is the degree to which this same creative sculpting is at work in our relationship to things around us as well as within us, how for each of us our habits of movement and perception and sensibility are continually structuring *all* of our reality. This is not a new thought— mystics and Buddhists and poets have been saying it for centuries—but it is a difficult one because it so utterly defies appearances and our common-sense beliefs. There is, after all, a world out there, and it is the business of my nervous system to inform me about it. And if I am reacting appropriately to that information, that is, if I am managing to survive, then the information clearly must correspond to reality.

But the truth is—and this is a truth about the nature and limits of human knowledge, not about the nature of the universe—whatever may be the case with objects and events "out there," the only thing about which I have any kind of direct knowing is the field of my personal perception, my conscious levels of awareness about what is happening in my body and its perceptual processes. The rest of the world as I know it is made up of my accumulating experiences of perception, inferences based upon them, and projections.

Projections based on desire, expectations based on past experience, beliefs about what is and is not possible, psychotropic chemicals, a wide variety of temporary distortions of perceptual networks—all of these can color our picture of reality (including both the image and the actuality of my body) in ways that are thorough and profound. What is more elusive is the fact that these conditions and processes are *continually* operative in one way or another, that they not only produce occasional distortions but are always inescapable elements in the tissue of our world. As William Blake said, "A fool sees not the same tree that a wise man sees." Under the most optimal conditions of clarity the best that we can say is that we are confronted with an irreducible ambiguity in every perception: the external object or event, and what my perceptions are making of it at the time.

Now here we come upon a very peculiar dichotomy about how to think about the thing we are thinking with. On the one hand, in the midst of the reality of our rich mental world, it is difficult to grasp and admit to ourselves what the brain *is*: A physical thing from which consciousness—all human consciousness of everything whatever—emerges, biochemical generator and integrator of all images, objects, sensations, thoughts, visions, and memories. Even all our ineffable experiences occur within brains. Revelation is a shift in firing patterns, and the experience of God-consciousness, insofar as we are personally aware of it, is itself a brain state. I may have *lived* a past life, but my present knowledge of that circumstance is a series of *current* brain states that reports it to—that *is*—my awareness. What is emerging into my attention from my information transduction system is *all that I can know*. Even inspired speculation about other possibilities—even the actual experience of those possibilities—is taking place within the collective activities of a living brain.

On the other hand, in a more clinical frame of mind, scientists want to make the brain account for *more* than it can do on its own. In our functional model of the human being we have assigned *all* roles of information gathering, processing, and transferring to assemblies of neurons. This overlooks the fact that many other systems in our bodies contribute many different kinds of information and integrated processes that add significantly to the content and tonality of our experience of consciousness. For instance: The circulatory system is heavily laden with chemicals carrying information as well as with oxygen and glucose; the entire connective tissue matrix is a semi-conducting medium which transmits electrical messages throughout the system; not only neurons but many kinds of tissues produce and receive neuropeptides; immune cells are roving information gatherers that report to the brain about invaders far too small for the neural sensorium to register.

The *entire soma* is, in a genuinely functional sense, brain. And *mind*, the contents of my mental field, is what all of these elements are doing together at any particular time. It is no coincidence that our stunted scientific and philosophical theories about consciousness have for the most part been written by people sitting in chairs, with no movements to set the somatic elements of mind into conscious motion.

There is probably enough in these notions to offend just about everyone. For materialists, the existential primacy of consciousness is far too slippery a concept, a world of fantasies and ghosts. For mystics, the idea that the perception of the over-whelming power and pervasiveness of consciousness is a phe-nomena inherently tied to the fragile biological matrix of a particular living organism composed of matter is equally un-acceptable.

But let us for a few moments suspend the beliefs of both, let us neither assume that this is the only deterministic world possible nor that it is the best of all possible beneficent worlds, but rather assume that it is the only world we have at the moment, and that all we know about it is what we are experi-encing as individuals right now. Some of the consequences of such a line of thought may be heady and terrifying, but let us try to avoid both false humility and overwrought hubris, and take courage in remembering that no bird soars too high if it soars on its own wings.

Human beings have discovered all the agreed upon scien-tific insights and have painted all the faces of God. Men and women have both adapted to the environment and destroyed it. They have engineered every social success and failure. They have solved the problems that have come their way, and they have created problems that never would have existed without them. They have captured the sacred fire of consciousness, and now they alternatively warm and burn themselves with it. Men and women have had all the visions, experienced all the revelations, written all the scriptures, devised all the prac-tices for enlightenment, and they have also fashioned all the torments of evil and ignorance that we know about.

There is no ultimate discovery or final theory that will for-ever complete our factual knowledge of the world. There is no coming revelation that will set all history right and ensure an unblemished future. Apocalypse, alien invasion and addi-tional lifetimes may be optimistic points of view. No one is coming to save us from ourselves, and our only opportunity to save ourselves is now. No one else can tell us what we most need to know, and no one else can undo the damage already done. Heaven and Hell are not disembodied rewards and punishments awaiting us in an afterlife; they are the immediate consequences of every act. Karma will not get me in the end; it is the function of my awareness to make it clear to me that karma is getting me every moment. I do not do good in order to be rewarded later; I do good in order to experience the consequences of my actions *now*. And when I do evil, the engulfment of my life with the awareness I have done so is itself the immediate punishment.

We are not creative merely during states of an unusual and inflamed imagination. We are radically creative and free to make choices in every normal moment, spinning a world out of our consciousness. We are constantly giving appearance, arrangement, and meaning to everything we perceive, and everything we can imagine. We are—perhaps you have felt this coming—the angels. Potential within ourselves is the higher consciousness to which we have been appealing. We are the concrete substance from which this consciousness is emerging. But being an angel is of little consequence unless I find, and feel, and strengthen, and flap mightily my wings. We are the ones we have been waiting for.

Conventional wisdom has it that without a credible threat of punishment in an afterlife, and without its corporeal agents on Earth, there would be no check whatever to immoral, criminal, self-serving, destructive behavior. Never mind the fact that these corporeal agents have themselves been responsible for a great deal of immoral and destructive behavior in the course of history. But let us simply ask, what sort of self is served by short-sighted destructive behavior? For socially dependent creatures, "self interest" inherently includes the welfare of those who provide us with necessities and pleasures, and upon those who provide for our providers, and those that provided for them.

Altruism and morality, in other words, are simply the recognition of serving a larger, more inclusive self. In the end, tolerance is no more "noble" than refraining from cutting off my nose to spite my face. To put another before ourselves is a sublime act not because it signifies self-sacrifice, but because it signifies the identification of the other as a part of our selves.

Another way to put this is that no bodyworker can possibly massage anyone but themselves, and no one will benefit more from it than you. I have experienced few other contexts where this unity of feeling and purpose is as palpable and dramatic. "let flesh touch with flesh", said Faulkner, "and watch the fall of all the eggshell shibboleth of caste and color too."

Gerald Edelman, a contemporary Nobel Laureate neurologist, observes in his book *Bright Air, Brilliant Fire*, "Societies are in the hands either of the commercially powerful but spiritually empty or, to a lesser extent, in the hands of fanatical zealots under the sway of unscientific myths and emotion."

Let us as therapists and responsible angels strive to be neither.

"Perhaps," Edelman goes on, "when we understand and accept a scientific view of how our mind emerges in the world, a richer view of our nature and more lenient myths will serve us. How would mankind be affected by beliefs in a brain-based view of how we perceive and are made aware: What would be the result of accepting the ideas that each individual's 'spirit' is truly embodied; that it is precious *because* it is mortal and unpredictable in its creativity; that we must take a skeptical view of how much we can know; that understanding the psychic development of the young is crucial; that imagination and tolerance are linked; that we are at least all brothers and sisters at the level of evolutionary values; that while moral problems are universal, individual instances are necessarily solved, if at all, only by taking local history into account? Can persuasive morality be established under mortal conditions? This is one of the largest challenges of our time....A theory of action based on the notion of human freedom—just what was missing in the days of the Enlightenment—appears to be receiving more and more support from the scientific facts."

Those who touch so many others with their wings have a special responsibility, having found those wings a little sooner. Failure to do so would be failure to themselves. The fear and guilt and false humility that may prevent us are all too human; but human too are the transcendent joys which we seek. Walt Kelly once said, in the voice of Pogo the intrepid opossum, "We have met the enemy, and he is us." I am suggesting that the same can be said of the angels. "The brain," according to Emily Dickinson, "is just the weight of God." Somewhere in the middle ground between self-abnegation and egomania lies the ownership of who and what we truly are— the angels, who are talking to themselves. Are you listening?

7

Facilitated Segments: Biomechanics and Pathology

Gravity and Human Biomechanics

Our upright posture and bipedal locomotion has opened the door to many uniquely human capacities and advantages. But it has also created a particularly human and problematical relationship with gravity. Maintaining an optimally efficient distribution of the weights of our body parts through our support structure is for us a highly complicated balancing act, and the chronic stresses arising from elaborate compensations developed to support our imbalances in the midst of gravity's perpetual pull are responsible in one way or another for a large number of our and dysfunctions and diseases.

The truth of these proposals—and the surprising *extent* of their truth—is obvious to anyone who has experienced for themselves the shift from a poor to an improved relationship with gravity. And yet they are met with skepticism, and even derision, within the mainstream models of the nature of health and disease. It is rather bewildering why the advocates of a model of the human being as a collection of interactive mechanisms have actually placed so little emphasis upon our mechanical inefficiencies. It won't do to say that mechanical maladjustments are inconsequential compared to "real" diseases and traumas. Anyone genuinely familiar with machines knows better: A slight misalignment in an automobile's steering mechanism does not result in inconsequential damage after several hundred miles of hard driving.

The Facilitated Segment

One of the more dramatic and well-researched examples of the impact of muscular patterns of posture and movement upon the central nervous system—and hence upon the functional integration of the entire organism—is a phenomenon referred to in osteopathic literature as the "facilitated segment," or "osteopathic lesion." The following information was drawn from *The Collected Papers of Irwin M. Korr*, teacher and research fellow at the Kirksville College of Osteopathic Medicine from 1945 to the late 1970's. This collection is published by The American Academy of Osteopathy, 2630 Airport Road, Colorado Springs, Colorado, and is readily available. The reader is encouraged to peruse it for more detail, as well as for a review of Dr. Korr's rigorous experimental methods and the well-reasoned arguments behind his conclusions.

Successfully adaptive movements of all kinds must take into account an enormous array of internal and external information. To this end, each motor nerve leaving the cord receives up to 15,000 synaptic connections from every conceivable source—the special senses, equilibrium centers, the muscle spindles and Golgi tendon organs, joint receptors, voluntary commands from the cortex, reflex organization from the midbrain and brain stem, sensory input from the autonomic system, and emotional tones from the hypothalamus and limbic system.

Both excitatory and inhibitory interneurons tie all of these elements together in each spinal segment, and connect each segment to others north and south, making for an almost infinite variety of combinations and isolations possible as the brain plays upon the individual tones and combined chords available on this spinal keyboard. If all the keys and connections are equally available and correctly responding to shifting circumstances, then all conceivable "kinetic melodies"—specific patterns of movement and behavior—are possible.

Now one of the principle features of these dense interconnections, balanced between excitatory and inhibitory, is that under normal operations no one source or impulse is adequate to fire a motor nerve and initiate a muscular contraction. Many impulses must converge at once, building up to a threshold of potential excitation, before any voluntary or reflex command springs the terminal motor nerves—the ones actually connected to relevant motor units and muscular groups—into action. This insures that motor nerves and muscular activity are insulated from the ongoing barrage of any and all stimulation, preventing us from becoming a perpetual spasm of disorganized reactions.

Dynamic give and take within and among segmental regions is necessary to adaptive function, and one form of pathology or another is the result of any segment remaining either inhibited or highly stimulated for too long a time. It is as though a key on the piano were either stuck and silent, or played fortissimo every time we gave it the slightest touch. Dr. Korr's research has to do with the potential chain of events that can, and to one degree or another always does, occur when a segment of the spinal cord is overstimulated over long periods of time by any of the many sensory or motor sources that converge upon it, "facilitating" its pool of interneurons to lower and lower thresholds of reaction.

The Osteopathic "Lesion"

Normally the term "lesion" refers to highly localized and specific *structural damage* in one tissue or another—a cut, a break, a cell death. The "osteopathic lesion" is quite different. All the localized neurons involved remain intact and operational; it is the nature of their *function* that is disturbed, primarily by overstimulation which leads to hyperexcitability and continual, spontaneous firing patterns. This is the main reason why it has so often eluded clear clinical recognition and definition, research attention, and therapeutic application—there is no visible structural alteration in the affected tissue. Nevertheless, its invisible hyperactivity and lack of synchronization with other crucial processes coordinated by the central nervous system generates pernicious effects that are readily observable and seriously debilitating, even though many of them may not have any initially obvious connection to the "lesion" itself.

Experimentally, Dr. Korr and his associates were able to produce facilitated, or lesioned, segments of the spinal cord with a revealingly simple technique: A clamping devise was placed on two lateral process of adjacent vertebrae, say T6 and T7. The clamp was then tightened slowly to increase local pressure on the nerve trunk and related tissues entering the spinal cord through the opening between the two vertebrae. Pressure was increased until the irritation it caused bombarded the cord's local interneurons with enough stimulation to significantly lower the threshold of these neurons to reactivity, facilitating them to a state of hyperexcitability as measured by their spontaneous firings detected by fine electrodes planted in the cord segment.

This clamping is analogous to the pressure put upon spinal nerve trunks by unbalanced body parts or chronic muscular contractions which impinge on any specific segment of the spine. And the irritation of the nerve trunk at this juncture can produce a wide variety of peripheral symptoms in any of the tissues that are synapsed to the sensorimotor or autonomic axons it bundles together. The spinal irritation may appear as "referred pain" in skin, muscles, organs or glands connected to the irritated segment of the cord. Incoming sensory messages can be confused and distorted, highly amplified by interneurons already "on edge" from overstimulation. Or motor signals may be similarly distorted on their way to muscle cells, causing increased tonus, over-reaction, or poor coordination.

These sensorimotor effects can be disturbing enough. However, they are relatively minor compared to the potential ramifications within the cord segment itself and its related autonomic ganglia. Once initiated, the facilitated segment can become one of the sensorimotor system's most vicious circles.

Once the squeeze on the T6 nerve trunk has been increased to a critical threshold, it requires only the slightest additional nudge to set off cascades of neural activity in its related segment. Amplified and distorted sensory messages are sent to the brain, local reflexes are spontaneously aroused, and all muscles and organs activated by the segments motor nerves are in for a sustained period of overstimulation and exhaustion.

But the dominoes don't stop here. If we select a pair of vertebrae several segments away, say T9 and T10, and apply clamping to them as well, what we will find is that a very slight amount of pressure will elicit no activity in the T10 segment, but *will* set off a strong and sustained volley of activity in the already facilitated T6 segment. That is, minor stimulations which cause no reactions in this second segment are immediately routed to the *initially facilitated* segment, where they produce dramatic reactions, significantly adding to its already amplified activity.

Furthermore, any mental or emotional agitation will surface most readily as muscular and glandular expression within the facilitated segment's domain. "Rest activity"—muscular movements or twitches when the subject is in repose or asleep—are generated far more frequently in the facilitated segment. Even the steady rhythm of breathing can eventually be enough to launch rhythmic cascades of facilitated impulses, causing both pain and spasm.

Hence the facilitated segment is not so much a radiating *source* of hyperstimulation up and down the cord as it is a *lens* which tends to focus and magnify any and all background stimulation from all over the body into the local neurons, muscles, organs and glands that are already "on edge." Along with disorganized reflex muscular contractions, a number of other characteristics become manifest in related tissues: Alterations in skin texture, reduced circulation, temperature changes, lowered pain thresholds, and an increased vulnerability to exhaustion and disease.

It is worth noting that the main sources of this local stimulation—pain receptors, pressure receptors, muscle spindles and Golgi tendon organs and other proprioceptors—are for the most part *non-adapting* receptors. That is, they continue to produce stimulation as long as the mechanical conditions of stress are present in the form of chronic postural imbalance, repeated gestures, or increased tonus. Facilitation, in other words, tends to be self-exciting and self-regulating, a phenomenon with a life and a developmental agenda all its own once it is set into motion. Dr. Korr is careful to point out that the osteopathic lesion is not the direct *cause* of organic disease; it is one of many factors. But, he concludes, "It is a most important factor—it is a sensitizing factor, a predisposing factor, a localizing factor, a channelizing factor." Overstimulation and exhaustion set up almost any tissue to become fertile soil for the sprouting of disease agents of all kinds.

These self-perpetuating patterns of facilitation can also produce a startlingly faithful mimicry of disease states, so much so that both diagnosis and treatment can be very ambiguous. During the Finnish campaign in WW II several hundred soldiers were treated for pneumonia in an experiment that had remarkable results. More than one variety of pneumonia, caused by different pneumococci and typically responsive to different antibiotics, were included.

The treatment involved only the injection of *Novocain*, a local anesthetic, to a diamond-shaped region extending from C3 to T4 and covering the medial halves of the shoulder blades. If the treatment was given early, the usual result was rapid and uneventful recovery. In this experiment, the therapeutic effect appeared to depend far more on the site of application— that is, adjacent to the spinal segments that directly service the lungs and primary breathing muscles—than upon the normal pharmacological matching of specific drug to specific disease.

In other words, when treatment was early enough the analgesic prevention of segment facilitation was just as effective as antibiotics, and had the added advantage of being effective against a variety of different pneumococci.

Widening Circles of Effects

We know that the spinal cord, the most ancient portion of our central nervous system, is responsible for a great deal of the organization of all sensory input and all motor output. What Dr. Korr is pressing us to recognize is that by virtue of the very same functional interconnectedness among its structures it is active in organizing—or disorganizing—our responses to stress, trauma, and illness as well. There is a potent form of operant learning going on in the cord, and each of us assembles highly personalized reactions that evoke and orchestrate the constellation of symptoms aroused by any pathological threat. We all learn our individual ways of expressing illness.

And notice how many options there are for mischief in this interconnectedness. Poor posture may create gravitational pressure that irritates nerves that can facilitate their spinal segment; hyperstimulation is then radiated out to muscles, glands, and organs fed by that segment, exhausting them, disturbing the balance of internal processes, and rendering related parts of the system vulnerable to malfunction or disease. Inflamed tissue just about anywhere can initiate the same sort of spasm and pressure conditions if the irritation persists long enough to facilitate its segment's pool of neurons. Any disease or trauma that actually attacks an organ, a joint, a muscle, can be the source of irritation that creates facilitation (as in the case of the WWII tubercular patients) Any one of a large number of habits and discomforts can generate the sensorimotor overstimulation in the cord that either weakens the resistance of peripheral tissues or sets off a series of secondary and tertiary effects throughout the whole system which eventually emerge as the symptoms of a much broader, deeper, and more complex pathology.

Note also that the nature of this broader pathological process is *entirely independent of the nature of the original insult,* be it physical, biochemical, or microbial. Secondary and tertiary symptoms and dysfunctions do not proliferate and circulate like germs, but are routed and reinforced by the spontaneous activity of the nervous system itself, and the entire profile of pathology tends to be shaped by the operational relations between tissues, nerve trunks, and the organization of spinal segments with one another. And many of these operational conditions are patterns that have been learned and perpetuated by life experience. Hence, distress in a single organ can produce vastly different overall reactions in different individuals, or the same reactions in different individuals may have been generated by very different initial causes.

Eventually we can probably expect the development of diagnostic tools that are sufficiently sensitive and simple enough to use to explore and document these pockets of excessive neural activity and begin to relate them clinically to a wide variety of symptoms and conditions. What we have until then, and will have after, are trained human observation and skilled manipulation of tissues caught up in spasm. High levels of tonus and specifically distorted patterns of muscular contractions can indeed be effectively addressed by a number of methods.

Dr. Korr maintained, as his data indicates, that even though the muscular and segmental involvement may appear extraneous to the pathology in question, they are in fact a significant part of the body's adaptation to the situation, and play a significant role in the perpetuation of the original problem and in the spreading of a whole constellation of reactive and compensatory problems in its wake. This reactive muscular and spinal element in the pathological complex is often the most assessable one, the one that can be effectively alleviated with a minimum of chemical or physical intrusion. And while it may not be the "cause" of the primary condition, it actively erodes the entire brain's and body's ability to combat it and restore balance and health. Removing these secondary obstacles to recovery are often decisive turning points in the process of regeneration, restoring the vitality and coordination necessary to the whole system in order to begin the deeper healing.

Significantly, Dr. Korr was careful not to claim any exclusivity for his own osteopathic—or any other—treatment modality for effective intervention. He speculated, and I believe correctly, that effective manipulation of the muscular component of segment facilitation will, "*in one form or another*," emerge as a dominant form of health care in the future. Indeed, just as chronic dysfunctional muscular contractions can trigger a wide variety of reactions, so are there a wide variety of approaches that can, in one way or another, successfully alter those patterns and establish more useful ones. Once a phenomenon has been acknowledged and defined, all sorts of other perspectives can be productively brought to bear upon it. Dr. Korr and his colleagues at Kirksville have articulated an elegant clinical model that is of enormous relevance to the entire field of somatic education.

8

Muscles and Emotions

Human biology—and by logical extension all of health care—is one science that cannot factor out emotions from its clinical investigations. In fact, the elimination of emotion from considerations of human development, behavior, pathology and healing is nothing short of a theoretical catastrophe. This is true simply because humans continually *have* emotions; they are like the weather—there is never a moment when we do not have one kind or another. And the specific nature of those emotions have profound and lasting impacts upon a vast array of physiological processes that are at work within our bodies, and which define in many ways our vitality, performance, biochemical balances, and overall state of health.

Yes, scientists or bodyworkers may distort observations and arrive at distorted conclusions due to the emotional ways they may fabricate theories and observe events. This is a very good reason, essential to the scientific method, for factoring out emotional responses as we gather and sift information. But what is different in biological research from that of pure physics or chemistry is the non-negotiable fact that emotions are a very significant *part of the data* that needs to be taken into account, whether our concern is learning, performance, healthy development or disease.

Indeed, the flattening of feelings itself is not an escape from emotions; it is the conscious adoption of a "flat affect," an emotional state which, like all others, is valuable for certain pursuits and not very useful in others. In other words, we may be able to achieve a high degree of objectivity in our understanding of how emotions work, but we are never free to disengage ourselves as living organisms from their perpetual presence within us and their effects upon us.

We are always having one feeling or another. There is no mental state that does not include the psychological and physiological elements we mean when we say "emotion" or "affect." And further, it is not possible to have an affect without triggering a range of biochemical and muscular responses within our organisms. This means that how we *feel* about ourselves and what is happening to us has at least as much—and sometimes more—to do with our health and happiness as do the physical events that are happening. That is to say, the emotions we are having at any given time are among the concrete events that are occurring. We may strive to filter out distorting sorts of emotions from scientific methodology, but we cannot banish from our lives the constant effect that any and all emotions are having upon us.

Imagine that you have played the piano for many years, and it is immensely gratifying as a secure, healthy and nourishing part of your identity. Your piano is in your private study, with everything arranged exactly as you want it to assist your state of mind when practicing—orderly, quiet and calm. In this space you have developed your skill for marvelous renditions of Chopin's *Nocturnes*—every nuance of tone and tempo, volume and color. The motor pattern you have established are at this point honed and stabilized into highly reliable reactions that flow through your fingers flawlessly each time you repeat a favorite piece.

Then during a large holiday dinner, your mother suddenly drags you to the downstairs piano and announces to all that you will now produce one of your beautiful *Nocturnes* for everyone to enjoy.

What is very likely to happen to your finely honed motor patterns? Notes are wrong, tempos falter, dynamics are muddled, nuances fractured. You struggle to the end without a hint of the gratification inherent in your relationship with your piano and with Chopin. Your mood is darkened, your conversation perfunctory for the rest of the party, and that night you do not digest your dinner at all well.

Were your skills somehow deprogrammed or wiped out? No, they will be waiting for you again in your study. But what was clearly and painfully observable is that they were knocked into utter disarray for the time being by conflicting emotions. The sudden shift in feeling state was enough to overwhelm years of faithful practice. And not only your playing suffered, but also your self-esteem, your social skills, and your digestion. And just possibly, some part of your relationship with your mother.

Whatever our specific skills, we have all had experiences similar to this crisis of motor performance, and felt the helplessness when our emotions alter our minds and disturb our performance. The entire musculature reacts to the feeling state of the moment. And if we pause to consider all of the things that accurate muscular coordination do or facilitate for us— that is, just about everything we do with our skeletal muscles, our gut tube, our circulatory system, our glands, our sexual responses or the fine tuning of our special senses to name a few—then the significance of these kinds of experiences deepens. Far more is at stake than a transitory embarrassing discomfort.

And many more kinds of responses in addition to carefully acquired and personalized motor skills like piano playing are involved. Many dimensions of my biological existence hinge directly upon complexly orchestrated muscle actions, and when they are scrambled by conflicting feelings, many of the life-supporting rhythms and harmonies become just as disorganized as did that Chopin performance.

For instance, the neural and chemical shock wave that courses through the body during the protective "Flight or Fight" response alters a large variety of internal activities: Blood pressure rises, circulation is shunted away from digestive organs to the skeletal muscles, clotting factors rise, pulse increases, pupils dilate, metabolic machinery shifts to convert stores of glycogen and various proteins to quickly make available more blood sugar, water retention mechanisms are thrown into gear, a collection of different glandular sphincters open and close and the sympathetic nervous system is strongly stimulated as a whole. In other words, a powerfully punctuated fear reaction shifts chemical balances, neural activities, and organ functions throughout the organism to help it to better deal with a current emergency.

But if, either under laboratory conditions or in real life experiences, these same widespread physiological reactions are sustained over long periods of time by stress and fear, they eventually deplete stores of fuel, waste a great deal of metabolic energy, exhaust glands and organs and uselessly maintains a psychological state of vigilance that interferes with virtually all levels of performance. Rather than preparing the animal for a current emergency, the over-stimulated protective responses themselves become an internal chronic "emergency," one which undermines the very mechanisms nature designed combat emergencies in general.

And more than that, if this stress and over-stimulation is continued long enough, the "Flight or Fight" mechanisms themselves can be permanently impaired: They become very sluggish in their response to real-time situations; the animal cannot successfully rally its resources to meet new challenges, and the blood chemistry of adrenaline and cortisol is permanently heightened, wreaking the same sorts of organic damage as chronic use of artificial stimulants and long-term dosages of cortisone.

Not only our own emotions, but those that are either lavished upon us or withheld from us have the same surprising degree of biological impact. Experiencing the love and concern of others, for instance, can have a dramatically therapeutic influence:

> All the pills and surgery that the medical profession can provide often will not work their full scientific magic without the *element of human caring*. Lisa Berkman, an epidemiologist and public health specialist at the Yale Medical School, monitored 200 older men and women who suffered heart attacks and found that those with the most support from others lived the longest after their attacks. Of those in the group studied by Berkman, *53 percent* with no close personal support died within six months, compared with *36 percent* of those with one source of support and *23 percent* of those with at least two people to care for them. While all that companionship and support may provide an obvious psychological boost, Berkman said solicitude contributes to healing *because of its physical effects*. "If you feel like you have emotional support, you may be less stressed," she said. "Your blood pressure doesn't shoot up, and your heart doesn't race." [Quoted from the *San Francisco Chronicle*, Friday January 20, 1995, page A26; emphases added.]

Fortunately—and this is one of the foundations of many kinds of "alternative" forms of health care—it is not always necessary to passively suffer either the spontaneous occurrence of an emotion within us or to wait upon emotions that may or may not be coming to us from others. Feeling states can be *actively cultivated* as well; we can learn to consciously flex their physiological and biochemical "muscles," and reinforce positive reactions in our bodies to wrestle with the potentially negative ones. We can actively learn to develop our emotional skill, our "emotional I.Q."

One of these positive feeling states—and one of the most promising in its potential for health and healing—has been extensively documented: the "Relaxation Response" investigated by Dr. Herbert Benson. Deep states of mediation, states that can be successfully learned and voluntarily evoked in as little as two weeks, produce a series of physiological, biochemical, and psychological responses that is as impressive as those occurring in the chain of "Fight or Flight" reactions. Stimulation of the sympathetic nervous system is dampened and the restorative parasympathetic system increases its activity. Pulse rate slows, and blood pressure drops. Arteries adjust their diameters to shunt blood away from the skeletal muscles to the gut tube; metabolic activity shifts away from consuming the body's stored resources and towards the absorption of new nourishment. Adrenaline and cortisol are removed from the blood stream, and an observable calmness replaces the hyper-vigilance of emergency or stress. These effects are the physiological elements of the feeling state of calm alertness, and they can no more be separated from the conscious experience of that calm than can the emergency responses following the sudden rush of fear or anxiety. These are the nuts and bolts of affect, and they are the concrete reasons why "calm" *feels better* than "anxious."

Moreover, we have so far documented only two emotional states; there are of course scores, and each of them contributes an array of physiological responses similar in scope but different in detail from those of fear or calm. One of the greatest discoveries in recent history concerning the links between feelings and bodily functions has been the identification of the *neuropeptides*, specific chemicals that are produced by the brain and by many other tissues to regulate the fusion of our mental and physical lives. So far about eighty of these chemical messengers have been discovered and tested; Candace Pert, their discoverer, estimates that there may well be as many as three hundred. Each of them produces a wide range of cellular and organ responses, and Pert maintains that there is great potential for their actions to be extremely significant for health and healing.

It has been established that a dominant and powerful locus for these chemically induced responses is the *hippocampus*, a structure that is a part of the *limbic*, or emotional centers, deep within the core of the brain. This is the area where the most bonding sites for neuropeptides exist, and the area from which their multitudes of mental, chemical, neural, physiological, and muscular reactions are projected out to the rest of the brain and the body. Its strategic location and its neural and circulatory links with other crucial brain structures in the immediate area is pregnant with suggestions about the specific ways feelings exert their influences in all the body tissues and processes.

The hippocampus is very close to the optic nerve tract, and hence linked to visual consciousness: I *see* a threat or a desired object, and all my visceral and muscular reflexes are engaged for the proper responses in either case; or, alternative, I am under the neuropeptide influence of a strong emotion, and this colors the ways I see and interpret the significance of what I am observing. Here is where I keep both my funky outlook and my rose-colored glasses.

The hippocampus is also closely related to the hypothalamus and pituitary gland, which together orchestrate most of the important hormonal rhythms of my entire organism. We see this connection in vivid action when a perceived threat launches the adrenaline, cortisol, and other hormones that in turn set in motion all of the "Fight or Flight" reactions. And we can infer that many other feeling states have similarly global hormone-monitoring effects.

This same area is where subconscious sensory processing areas are located, where incoming information undergoes an important organization before it is passed on to the cortex. In particular, here is where a great deal of my proprioceptive sensations are assembled into a coherent *body image*—my partly objective and partly subjective sense of my shape, size, position in space and my internal parts. Naturally, this is crucial data that underlies the decisions I make regarding all kinds of gestures and postures, analyses of what is possible for me to do and what is not, and specific sequences and strategies with which to accomplish any particular movement. This body image is subject to all manner of emotionally related distortions, such as the anorexic's self-perception of fatness, or the blank spaces in our body map that result from the emotional repression of troublesome body parts, suppression or heightening of local symptoms, and so on. From these distortions of feelings and beliefs come a legion of limitations and of inappropriate habits and responses.

The highest processing ganglions of the autonomic nervous system, which orchestrate all of the visceral, smooth-muscle organs of the body, are also located close to the hippocampus. Here is a major junction between my current feeling state, my past experience, and a wide range of autonomic reactions. This is the relay station that converts anxiety into ulcers, fear into impotence, anger into flushing, anticipation into sweaty palms, desire into a throbbing heart. It is also the place where the organism's deep biological needs are translated into emotional reactions to events and objects in our perceptual field, greatly enhancing and enriching the formation of behaviors built around acquisition or avoidance—finer and finer distinctions between what is good for us and what is bad. Some of the clearest and most documented relationships between the body and the mind are these correspondences between emotional states and visceral functions, and a few internal influences are more potent, for better or for worse, to the overall development of a healthy organism.

The pituitary and hypothalamus, densely linked to the hippocampus, are also responsible for a large amount of the activity that alerts and monitors the *immune system*. The body's overall immune defenses are profoundly affected by the mind's feeling states. This was clear in Lisa Berkman's study of elderly heart attack victims, and it has been demonstrated in countless other ways: Animals that have received affection in the lab are far more resistant to toxins and stresses; animals that have severely reduced stimulation in their environment fail to respond appropriately to many kinds of assaults on their systems. There is, in fact, a very close and now documented connection between mental state, neuropeptide secretions, and the chromosomal expression of specific proteins in white blood cells that "turn on"—or fail to turn on—their attack responses aimed at specific invaders.

Finally—and most directly related to our skeletal muscle reactions and learned patterns—the hippocampus is connected with the upper brain stem and the basal ganglia, the highest organizational level of the *gamma* sensorimotor system. These are the centers in which reflexes are orchestrated to coordinate virtually all of my skeletal muscle activity, from breathing, swallowing and gravitational reflexes to the development of locomotion patterns and all other acquired skills. This is where the Chopin performance went haywire when jangled nerves clashed with a carefully developed skill. And it is also where a state of calm alertness readies our muscles for optimal learning, split-second timing and graceful execution.

In our time it is the alternative and somatic therapeutic approaches that have most consciously and most effectively addressed these critical emotional components of self-organizaton, perception, and behavior. Soothing sounds, colors, smells, tactile stimulation, energy field manipulation, structural interventions, and movement repatterning all can contribute powerfully in their individual ways to more efficient and productive links between emotions and all of the muscles of the body—skeletal, smooth, and cardiac alike.

These approaches work because of a fundamental ambiguity in the body's and the mind's fields of experience between qualities of *sensory* feelings and the qualities of *emotional* feelings. Pleasing, nourishing contact of all kinds sets into motion the biochemistry and physiological processes that are the underpinning and the concrete expression of positive emotional feeling states, and these positive states in turn are fed forward into all of the processes that regulate the cortical, autonomic, limbic, and brain stem activities that organize all behavior for better or for worse.

Approaches and techniques that have made this kind of positive intervention possible have developed because these alternative therapists have taken feelings seriously. And more than that, they have treated them not merely as data, scientifically interesting in their own right, but have cherished them, listened to them for their wisdom, cultivated them, and discovered ways to pass them on to other organisms. They have made great strides in learning the rules of the biological causes and effects of these emotions. This is one of the main reasons that bodywork and many other alternative approaches will be such a large part of the health care—and the education—of the future.

9

Beyond the Brain:
A Body of Information

Universal Entropy

As one popular theory has it, Creation—both in its planetary and cosmic aspects around you and its biological aspects within you—is relentlessly running down. Since the Big Bang, all physical processes have been steadily using up all available energy, a constant diminishment referred to as "entropy." Everything is ever-more closely approaching an eternal inertness when there will no longer be sufficient force left to animate all the events of the universe and all the processes of our bodies.

All the stars are consuming themselves. All thermal systems are cooling towards absolute zero. Gravity is steadily slowing the expansion of the cosmos, and this loss of universal momentum is further increased by innumerable frictions and impacts. All wave forms are dispersing into fainter and fainter and eventually undetectable fields. All orbiting objects are slowly falling in towards their centers of attraction, all surface are being eroded, and all liquids are seeking the final stasis of their lowest possible level of containment. All organic compounds are continually breaking down into simpler constituents, all tissues are aging and degenerating, and all organisms are dying. With every tick, time's own clock is winding down the spring that drives its mechanism, and with every passing moment your mind is inching towards senility, dementia, and eventual silence.

All these gloomy predictions are logically inevitable the moment one acknowledges a world made up of solid objects interacting like billiard balls, losing angular momentum with each new contact and rebound. The emotional and conceptual forces of these beliefs are enormous and pervasive, and they silently underlie a great many of our scientific, historical, and biological assumptions about the nature of disease and death, the trajectory of human progress, the development of social values, and so on.

For instance: There once was a Golden Age, the "Good Old Days" when everything was newer, stronger, better; now that Age is irrecoverably past. Youth is the most active—and most attractive—time of life. Every trauma or disease further weakens the system. After a relatively early apex of growth and vitality, all living is dying. The painful and humiliating degenerations of old age are unavoidable. All social revolutions begin in an excess of naive enthusiasm and end in the same old inertia and decadence. It doesn't really matter who is in charge or what changes are promised, because the problem is an irreparably degenerate system. Conservation doesn't matter in the long run, because we need to use it all up before it's gone anyway. The maintenance of health has primarily to do with the balancing of chemicals and the repair—or removal—of dysfunctioning pieces and parts. What we cant' cure, we simply have to endure.

And, in order to avoid the paralysing depression this world view naturally begins to foster, we characterize these negative expectations as "pragmatic realism," sailing into their self-fulfilling prophesies with a sort of plucky existential pride that allows us to carry on in spite of them.

Universe as Information

There is, however, another way to view this entire situation, a model which suggests altogether more open-ended possibilities of development and a self-renewing source of sustained—even increased—energy that keeps the cosmos and life on our planet humming. Objects bouncing off one another dissipate their kinetic energy and eventually reach a state of zero momentum. But what if "objects" were not just "things" that "bounce off" each other? What if we regarded objects as essentially temporary and provisional assemblages of *information*, information encoded as fields, as atomic vibratory rates, as molecular packages whose shapes and distribution of charges have specific significance and "meaning" (i.e., functional possibilities) for all the other molecules around them?

This is the foundation of the theory of the *universe as information system*, rather than as essentially inert and meaningless objects of various sizes and types. And it is a point of view that stimulates profoundly different consequences than do the assumptions of the entropy theory.

Information does not run down. Its operations are not eternally defined by a fixed number of physical laws. Information combines and recombines with other information to continually create novel formations and reactions: Forms *in*form other forms, and generate new in*form*ation. The cosmos is not a three-dimensional billiard game in which all the balls are steadily running out of steam. It is a vast, intelligent, and autodidactic *conversation*, in which all information evokes new information.

A world of ramifying and accumulating information is one far different from a "merely" material one that is winding down according to known laws of cause and effect. It is a world of continually changing contexts, shifting significances, and expanding possibilities. Most especially, it is a world that is not condemned by the principle of physical entropy to an end foreseeable within the conditions present at the very beginning. Rather it is a world that is continually reorganized by a principle of *emergence*, in which new resolutions, new contexts, and subsequently new problems are continually appearing that could never have been realized in states prior to the contemporary ones in which they first appear. It is all a great deal more like thinking and learning than it is like impacting and rebounding. Things are not winding down, but are constantly reorganizing themselves into higher, more complex, and more energetically potent situations.

Information, Body, and Mind

Now one of the long-standing impediments to thinking coherently about this curious combination of physics, chemistry, and psychology that we call human life has been the belief that "form" is purely physical and exists exclusively in the domain of the material body, while "information" is purely mental, non-physical, and exclusive to mind.

Furthermore, "mind" has itself been defined as simply an epiphenomenon—a side-effect—of the physical operations of the brain, and can have no concrete effect on the material processes of our bodies. This is to say that your mental experience of your life, being immaterial, has no quantifiable impact whatever upon the concrete course of your physical development, your states of health and disease, and the nature of your eventual demise. The body, and with it its passive "epiphenomenon" the mind, is doomed to entropy.

But again, all this changes quite drastically if we stop viewing the body as a collection of "objects," and begin experiencing it as a grouping of forms which inform one another and interact to create new formations that in turn generate new information. If form and information amount to the same thing, which after all is what words and syntax are all about, then body and mind can never be exclusive domains. My body is simply the shape with which my being has been informed; and my mind is simply the ongoing management of all the information that is invested in every cell, tissue, organ, and system.

Brain vs. Mind

Another serious consequence of strictly separating "objects" and "information" has been the enduring notion that thoughts, feelings, habits, memories, learning, orchestrated reactions, and other manifestations of "intelligence" can only occur in a limited and highly specialized part of the body—the nervous system. To the degree that "mind" is even admissible in scientific biological discussion, it is typically relegated to the activities of brain, all other tissues and processes being purely physical phenomena that are monitored or directed by the computational and communicative functions of neurons.

This is an unnecessarily specialized and stunted idea of "intelligence." Not that I would trivialize or detract from the astonishing dimensions of intelligence obviously produced by the human brain; no computer offers even a meaningful point of comparison. But can it really be true that the brain is the only object in the universe, or in my body for that matter, that manifests intelligence? What do we actually mean by "intelligence," anyway? And how exactly is it different from the "cause and effect' sequences determined by the laws of physics and chemistry? And how can it be that it never existed in any form prior to recent and specific evolutionary developments in mammalian, or perhaps only in primate brains?

After all, rubber bands have "memory." They remember how long they are supposed to be when released. Complex organic proteins have "motor programs" that allow them to fold up in a long and faithfully repeated sequence to obtain their final shape. Crystalline formations "learn" how to precipitate faster and faster once an initial seed forms successfully. These are not merely metaphors, but are instances of observed "behavior." Why should we credit with intelligence only those instances that occur in higher organisms with specifically evolved brains? And how, in the end, does relegating all these cognitive operations to brains—complex objects—

help us to reinforce a world view in which objects do not, cannot have intelligence?

Many Informational Systems At Work

If what we mean by intelligence is the reliable encoding, storage, retrieval, communication, and recombination of specific data then it seems obvious that intelligence is occurring around us all the time, that it in fact is an intelligent universe.

The truth is that there are a large number of coherent and self-regulatory informational systems operating in my body, transferring an enormous array of data back and forth and transducing it from one system to another continually. Neurons are only the latest means of communication and response in biological organisms. Evolution has captured and preserved and continued to utilize every trick of information management that an information universe has provided.

1. ENERGY FIELDS. Waves emanating from a source are precisely expressive of the activities of that source. And they are interactive with all other waves they encounter and with all other sources they contact. In this sense every one of my organs is like a radio station, broadcasting through various wave mediums in and around me their current news, commentary, weather, and sports. Every other organ is listening, and responding.

Physisists now postulate that all objects and events are the results of various wave fields intersecting and reinforcing one another in specific ways, so it seems likely that this encoded wave principle of communication and recombination underlies virtually all other forms of intelligence in our bodies. And since we are essentially a fluid medium ourselves—75% water—we are ideally suited to imprint, to generate, and to transfer all sorts of wave forms with nearly perfect efficiency and accuracy. Every jiggle of our internal water balloons sends out cascades of these waves and every cell responds to their collective rhthyms.

2. MOLECULAR FORMS AND FUNCTIONS. Molecules are complex packets of form and function, already manifesting some of the characteristics of miniature "bodies" and "minds." The push and pull of atomic forces from which they are assembled create and maintain specific overall shapes, define specific interior domains with specific energetic properties, connect these domains into coherent structures capable both of repetitive interaction and further development, establish external points of interaction with other molecules, and define shapes of movement that the whole aggregate can make within its environment. Every change in content or structure alters the physical and energetic configuration—hence the potential function and "meaning" of a molecule; they are not piled together like bricks, but mutually evolved like relationships. Some of the more complex ones, like RNA, can even reproduce themselves.

They are energetic ideograms that can be endlessly altered and combined to create new words and phrases in the language of matter. A dramatic testimony to their potential for information coding, storage, recombination, and retrieval is the recent development in computer technology which tags sequences of individual molecules to create recording and read-out codes. The resulting miniaturization of stored bits of information allows for vastly expanded amounts of data that can be contained and manipulated in much smaller storage devices. This is an inherent capacity in molecules themselves that we have learned to harness in a technological fashion, not a property that has just been synthesized.

3. CELL MEMBRANES. All life forms, no matter how primitive or how developed, begin with a coalescence of *identity*, the imposing of a barrier between the "me" and the "not me," a reliable boundary separating biological developments within

the living unit and the more disorganized raw materials of chemistry and physics on the outside. This is already an astonishing piece of self-responsive intelligence. But it is not enough to merely maintain this boundary. Necessary raw materials for growth and renewal have to be imported; toxins destructive to the life processes must be kept out; required ingredients must be contained, while the continual production of metabolic waste must be ejected.

All of these operations require specific, reliable, and accumulating ways of making crucial judgments about what is in what is out, what is good and what is bad in the ultimate biological sense. In this regard the membrane can be viewed as the "mem-brain" of the cell, tasting and regulating a complicated two-way flow of materials and information.

One of the primary mechanisms for this flow is a variety of "gate molecules" that become embedded in the membrane, forming pores that can open and close as entry/exit channels Their operation across the membranes already illustrates a molecular "reflex strategy" that can be observed in increasingly complex forms throughout evolution and individual development: Toxin—>Danger/Bad/Contract/Close/Avoid and Nourishment—>Help/Good/Expand/Open/Embrace.

4. CELL UNITS. In addition to highly discriminatory membranes, all cells have evolved a considerable variety of methods of receiving, sending, and processing information. Each cell is a small but full-fledged organism, with a set of organelles each responsible for different life functions, transport systems within the cell, a variety of internal structures sensitive to different chemical messengers, and with complicated sequences of activity to orchestrate.

And, of course, the nucleus of the cell is the storehouse for the DNA templates, which preserve the fundamental code sequences for all the proteins that the cell will be obliged to manufacture for growth, repair, and reproduction. This is the most stable long-term memory system in the body.

5. CIRCULATION AND NEUROPEPTIDES. One of the primary ways which cells and tissues use to communicate directly to one another is through the sending and receiving of tiny chemical messengers called neuropeptides. We think of our circulatory system primarily as the means by which oxygen and glucose are delivered to cells as fuel and by which metabolic waste is cleared. But in addition to these functions the blood, lymph, and intercellular fluids are teaming with scores of molecules that are specifically information-laden and activity-catalyzing for virtually all cells in the body.

We have long known about hormones that initiate various physiological states and events, and pheromones that trigger complex social behaviors. To this chemical repertoire must now be added over 80— and perhaps as many as 300—substances which have pronounced emotional, cognitive and functional effects.

When one of them attaches to a receptor molecule in the membrane of a target cell, they initiate one of a wide variety of possible chemical reactions within the whole cell, including the selection and reproduction of particular DNA sequences from the nucleus. If that target cell is a crucial link in a larger functional chain, the activity of the entire chain is significantly altered by the contact of one molecule with one cell. The target cell can in turn produce and release a responsive neuropeptide that can relay the net result of these events to additional target cells further down the circulatory line.

It now seems likely that this circulatory information system was an early form of an integrated sensorimotor and autonomic regulator, active long before neural networks had ever appeared. Bacteria colonies have been observed to orchestrate their collective behaviors in response to neuropeptides that are identical to some of those found in our bodies.

6. CONNECTIVE TISSUE. Collagen is one of the most ubiquitous proteins in the body. It enwraps everything and threads its way in and out of everywhere. It is generally thought of as

the binding, unifying fabric of the body. In this regard it is one of the chief elements in our overall shape, and this overall form is then one of the principal pieces of information concerning our body image and various bodily functions.

But this is scarcely even the beginning of the connective tissue matrix's capacity for information generation and transfer. Connective tissue is not just a binder; it is also a semiconductor of electricity. Semiconductors are very versatile, and in may ways more interesting than pure conductors. They not only carry electrical impulses along from here to there; they can also transform it in a large number of ways: The coil in a light bulb is a semiconductor that changes electricity to light; in a heater the coils change it into heat; in a transistor it can amplify or impede a signal; in a computer chip semiconductors can be elaborately circuited to create all sorts of gates, encoders, storage devices, and message transducers. Your own connective tissue matrix shares many of these kinds of qualities and functions.

In addition, this matrix not only conducts, but also self-generates electrical currents—it is a *piezo-electric* substance, one that creates polarities and current flow when it is bent, stretched or compressed. It has been speculated that this matrix of electrical generation and conduction is the medium through which acupuncture meridians channel their energetic flow. And since the matrix intimately encases everything, from major organs and structures to individual cells, it is perfectly situated to bundle together not only physical pieces and parts but many streams of information as well.

7. NERVES. We have been taught to think of the nervous system as the exclusive information system of the body, but as we have seen, there are many other kinds of biological information processors that were operating successfully long before the neural one appeared, even in its most primitive form. Nerves do present some powerful refinements upon earlier information systems: They harness energy fields with action

potentials across their membranes and channel these waves down their axons to specific targets, rather than radiating them in all directions. Thee action potentials are a new and sophisticated function of membranes, above and beyond monitoring the cells' boundaries.

Alternatively to the usual electrical circuit analogy, the nerve network could be regarded as a much-accelerated circulatory system, one that delivers specific molecules through a series of rapid relays rather than through a continuous tube activated by a single pump. Nerves are the most active producers, senders, and receivers of neuropeptides, which directly connects their information flow and responses to many other kinds of tissue in the body. Relative to connective tissue, they conduct their energy flow through circuits far more microscopic, more numerous, and more precisely mapped than the semiconductor meridians of connective tissue. But these functional advances notwithstanding, the neural network neither replaces nor diminishes the importance of all the other data coursing through all the other nested and layered information systems within our organisms. Every one of them contributes to our experience of consciousness and our biological functions.

Perhaps the real advance presented by nerves is their collective ability to transduce, collect, store, and process virtually *all* other forms of information in the body, allowing for a far more dense composite of data and a much faster means of orchestrating overall patterns in response to the input of any one source.

Bodywork As Information

Now, what should be obvious in this context to practitioners of all sorts of bodywork is that the introduction of any contact or movement—or even a specific shift in the focus of conscious attention—immediately initiates changes in the informational content of all of these biological communication systems. Indeed, there are many bodywork modalities that define themselves according to their manipulation of one or anther of these systems: energy fields, fluid pulsations, circulation, connective tissue resilience, posture and other aspect of body shape and organ placement, semiconductor effects, sensor experience, memories, and so on.

It seems to me that this is the crucial concept, one that is absolutely necessary to grasp if bodyworkers are to define their profession and its methods in scientifically meaningful and popularly understandable ways. The mainstream allopathy of our time primarily presumes a world of objects, pieces and parts to be added, removed or replaced in order to relieve concrete physical symptoms. Much has been accomplished in this fashion; every computational system has hardware that can break down. But a body is not just a collection of anatomical parts; it is a dynamic and continually evolving assembly of *information*. Information does not "break" and cannot be "fixed." It is partial or complete, confused or clear, correct or misleading. It can be augmented, amplified, reorganized, reevaluated, refined. Its conundrums are not repaired like a machine or a chip; they are solved like a puzzle. Even a child knows that a bad picture does not necessarily mean that the television needs to be repaired. More often than not it just needs to be adjusted—its information flows reorganized.

Nor, in an information world, do we have to resort to the paradoxes and unresolvable distinctions between "body" and "mind." All objects are assemblies of information; all coherent collections of information exhibit intelligent organizations; evolving new consolidations, combinations and developments of intelligence are what mind does. The brain is a a physical object; if it is capable of producing intelligence then no object can categorically be denied the potential for informational content. Indeed, *all* objects are continually seething with a self-regulating chaos of energy, motion and change. In the broadest—and most biologically relevant—sense of the term, the entire body is "thinking." And bodywork can so profoundly alter the shapes, internal relationships and process of the organism because it supplies what every self-regulating entity requires: New, more complete, and clearer information. Body-work is information. And in an informational universe it is no "alternative" to a scientific point of view. It is of the essence in a new science.

10

The Breath of Life

Milton Trager told his students for many years that his birth as a therapist was the moment when in 1924, as a sixteen-year-old working as a mail carrier in Miami, he spontaneously experienced his first fully conscious breath.

On the bulletin board on the way out of the mail employees' back room were posted weekly instructions and tips on self-care, to be read and duly initialed by all carriers. One week the instructions simply read, "Take a deep breath." The first day he saw it, Milton just initialed the message and moved on. But the second day, finding himself alone in the hallway, he paused. Setting his mail bag down, he stood up and breathed. Many years later he would say, "That was the beginning of me." He added,

> I'm not sure I understand even now why and how it happened that way, so quickly. I guess I was ready. After so long, I was ready. The right moment. For the first time I felt *me*. I was almost afraid to take another breath, afraid somebody would be there, laughing. But it was like I was invisible, and I plunged on. The sensation became fuller, stimulation at its best. I got higher and higher. And the important thing is, it stuck. The way a true discovery always does, I suppose. It was the first edge of all I was going to discover about my body and, through my body, about me.[1]

A breath is the first act of human life. It announces the independence of the new creature from the life-line of the mother; it is the embrace of a new reality, and the initiation of a rhythm that will continue until death.

The practice of a variety of kinds of breath is at the core of many disciplines, from the athlete's development of increased stamina to the perfect still point of the meditator. Yoga practices all over the world and throughout history have been developed to cultivate full and conscious breath. From rebirthing to conscious dying, from relaxation techniques to enlightenment, from asanas to frenzied activity, from gestalt therapy to pearl-diving, focus upon the act of breathing is the most common single thread in virtually all optimal performance.

The Chemistry of Breath

Reduced to its barest essentials, breathing is the gathering of oxygen into the organism and the expulsion of carbon dioxide, one of the principle waste products of metabolism. Even single celled organisms have to breathe in this sense, and so does every one of our six trillion individual cells within the body.

Breathing is a continual oxygen in-oxygen out activity, the life-giving element entering as O_2 and exiting as CO_2; we do not store it in any appreciable quantity, and this is why we must continually replenish the internal supply, why we must constantly maintain the rhythm of respiration. We tend to think of the constant supply of oxygen to be the important part of breathing, but the voiding of carbon dioxide is equally critical. In fact, we can go without inhaling oxygen for considerably longer than we can tolerate the build-up of CO_2. You have enough oxygen currently dissolved in your blood stream to keep your brain cells alive for eight to ten minutes; but it is the rising excess of carbon dioxide that makes you dizzy, desperate, and unconscious in a minute and a half or so.

This, by the way, is a very important thing to keep in mind when treating conditions like asthma. The asthmatic tends to have the illusion that there is not enough oxygen in the world, and gets caught up in a more and more labored *inhale*, creating the typical rigid barrel-chest of chronic asthma victims. But the more immediate truth is that there is altogether too much carbon dioxide in their world, and it is the complete deflation of a powerful *exhale* that they need most, both to vent the toxic waste gas and to empty out for the next intake of oxygen. Learning to empty out is the great act of faith that gives them the space to fill up again.

Once oxygen is taken up by a cell, it is transported to the internal organelles called *mitochondria*, the principle fuel refineries and energy dynamos of every individual cell. Within the chambers of the mitochondria, the molecules of oxygen combine in a complex chemical reaction with glucose, the basic blood-sugar to which most of what we have eaten has been reduced, and which has also been taken up by the cell and transported to the mitochondria. Glucose, the refined result of what we have eaten, is the primary fuel that is oxidized by what we have breathed, and this interaction is the tiny flame within the mitochondrian combustion chamber; this "Flame" provides the heat that keeps the cell at a living temperature and liberates the molecular energy locked within the fuel. And this is the energy necessary for all of the cell's life processes. This enzyme-regulated and self-perpetuating slow burn, called the Krebs Cycle, is the final fusion of digestion and respiration, and the initial stage of cell metabolism, which branches out in many directions and functions from this steady source of ready energy. Pyruvic acid produces two similar molecules at several places along the circular chain —$FADH_2$ and $NADH_2$. It is the interaction of these two molecules with oxygen that defines the critical place of oxygen in the life-sustaining energy cycle of the cell.

So the primary chemical-energetic role of oxygen, in combination with glucose in the Krebs Cycle, is to reconstitute the ATP fuel supply that is the specific source of energy for most ongoing life functions. Oxygen is crucial in the refining of the fuel for *metabolism*. An important corollary is that there cannot be a higher level of metabolism—life function—than there is a steady supply of oxygen to feed it. Glucose can be stored and these stores drawn upon for extended periods of time; oxygen must continually be imported, or the process immediately slows accordingly.

And breathing *is* the active importation of oxygen. So the effective volume of each breath is the limiting factor on the amount of life-function within the organism and its individual cells that can take place from moment to moment. Notice that "oxygen" is simply a word that we give to the atomic structure that supplies this energy to the cell's cycle. Somehow this functional relationship between oxygen and breathing is related to what is designated by "ch'i," "charge," and "life-force." Thus breath, in a variety of languages and a variety of cosmologies, constitutes a primary activity of life and is foundational in the development of consciousness. We cannot *be* more than we can *breathe*.

The Mechanics of Breath

We normally think of the diaphragm as the "breathing muscles;" and in fact, it is the largest *single* muscle of respiration. But truly effective breathing that can sustain ch'i, metabolism, and a high degree of physical activity is far more complicated than the action of one or a few muscles. If you stand up and create a forced exhale that empties your lungs as much as possible, and follow with a forced inhale that fills your lungs as much as possible, you will discover that you must collapse and extend your entire posture to do so, changing the position of almost every bone, and hence the length of almost every muscle in your body.

This means that in a full breath, or any significant fraction of it, most of the body's muscles participate in a carefully orchestrated movement that effectively expands and collapses the lung-chamber. If you observe a sleeping baby closely, you will see that all of its body is in rhythmical motion—chest rising and falling, abdomen rising and falling, arms and legs rolling out on the inhale and in on the exhale, even the spine lengthening and shortening. Therefor, the first breath that you took, free from the womb and the umbilical cord, was a perfectly orchestrated, complicated reflex movement that successfully organized almost all your muscles in a single action. And you got it right the first time—one of nature's great gifts, your very first birthday present.

And it may well be that that was the last time you got it exactly right—because every subsequent use of your muscles (resisting gravity, exploring, developing locomotion, modeling available examples, acquiring skills, compensating for injuries, and so on) is imposed upon this primary rhythm, and must utilize the same muscles at the same time. Many of these secondary movement patterns take on an importance and momentum of their own, and thus interfere with free and effective respiration.

These interferences typically develop slowly and unconsciously, so that we seldom notice their dramatic impact. But you can illustrate this impact easily for yourself: Stand erect, and take a comfortable deep breath. Mark to yourself the feeling of the volume of that breath. Then thrust you head out as far as you can (without hurting yourself, of course), and again—holding that head-thrust posture—take a deep breath. Note the radical diminishment of volume. Next, stand erect and then deepen your lumbar curve as much as possible, and again take a deep breath and compare its diminished volume to the original erect breath.

You can continue this experiment as you wish, using different exaggerated contractions in different body areas, and what you will consistently find is that any significant distortion of posture engages muscles that cannot be utilized in full breathing, compromising breath volume directly and dramatically.

And the chemical, energetic result of this is a lowered metabolism, lowered charge, lowered energy resource for virtually all other activities.

A Highly Habituated Pattern

Repetition is an extremely powerful principle. It is the little things that occur over and over that produce the greatest long-term effects, like grains of sand in the wind sculpting the entire landscape. And there is nothing you will repeat as many times in your muscular life as the rhythm and shape of an exhale and an inhale—approximately 20 times a minute, or 28,800 times a day. If each cycle of respiration is full and uninhibited, each breath continually reinforces the patterns of maximum charge for minimum effort. But if chronic postural, defensive, inhibitory, or compensatory patterns interfere, then each breath reinforces these distortions just as effectively, etching them deeper and deeper into our unconscious, becoming more and more permanent fixtures that place dramatic mechanical limits upon breath volume and potential life-charge for the entire organism, all 6 trillion cells.

And so far in our discussion this has only to do with *primary respiration*, the filling and emptying of the lungs. The cells in your big toe don't really care how full you can get your lungs, until you deliver the oxygen (and glucose) via the bloodstream to their specific locale. This delivery process is called *secondary respiration*, just as crucial as the primary, and just as dependent upon full, uninhibited muscular activity throughout the body.

The heart is a muscle about the size of your fist. If it has to generate the only force that pushes quarts of blood through hundreds of thousands of miles of circulatory piping, it will eventually exhaust itself. It requires the pumping assistance of all the body's muscles, expanding and contracting, pushing and pulling blood along as they shorten and lengthen, getting thicker and thinner, during normal activity. Every muscle in the body is potentially either a pump or a tourniquet for this fluid, life-giving circulation. Any chronic contraction is a dam; any chronic flaccidity is a stagnant bog in the flow of life out towards every living cell.

Further than this—no glucose or oxygen can reach a waiting cell until they *leave* the circulatory piping of arteries and capillaries. All nourishment must seep into the intercellular fluid before it can migrate to a cell membrane. And at this final, crucial stage of delivery via the flow of intercellular fluids around each cell colony, the overall muscular system is the *only* pump that is active; the heart no longer plays any role at all. So the very muscles that are actively engaged in movement are the same muscles that are helping to supply themselves with glucose and oxygen for the metabolic energy that will sustain that movement. And conversely, the very muscles that are caught in a chronic contraction, working hard but producing no motion, are the very muscles that are choking off their own supplies.

Notice that when things are working freely and cooperatively, the full-body motion of deep and uninhibited breathing is the same full-body motion that assists the heart and that circulates the intercellular fluid around cell colonies. And any additional movement, requiring more fuel and more oxygen, creates additional pumping which assists additional delivery. It is all quite cunningly designed to perfectly regulate and reinforce itself—until postural distortions, dysfunctional patterns, and chronic contractions become superimposed upon these primary operations.

Inspiring Respiration

In the context of this fundamental chemical/energetic life process, it is obvious what a crucial role effective bodywork has to play. Stress reduction, emotional calming, postural correction, movement re-education, range of motion improvement, relaxation are all common stocks in trade for most varieties of bodywork, and they all positively impact the muscular conditions in which respiration and all other activity take place.

When a balance is achieved between sufficient strength and resilience (not too much flaccidity) and sufficient economy of effort (no wasted or chronic contractions), then both primary and secondary respiration can effectively take in and circulate precious oxygen and clear away carbon dioxide—and all the other waste products of life.

Through this universal channel, bodywork can boost countless additional organic processes by addressing the dysfunctional muscular and mental patterns that life has unconsciously habituated in all of us. Every strengthening and every softening, and every improvement of coordination, is a movement towards life.

---

[1]Quoted from *Moving Medicine: The Life and Work of Milton Trager, MD.*, by Jack Liskin, 1995

II

Touch and Tolerance:
Bodywork As a Social Force

Rarely has keeping up with headlines and editorials been more disturbing than it has been lately. Yugoslavia. Chechnya. Oklahoma City, the World Trade Center. Civilian militias heavily armed with sophisticated weapons, inflamed by conspiracy theories. Religious fundamentalists and an angry right wing advocating—and escalating—a "holy war" to take back "our country." Widespread cynicism about the effectiveness of our government, reinforced by a polarized partisan political gridlock that does in fact seems wholly incapable of addressing acute problems with our economy, employment, education, welfare, health care, crime, civil rights, moral compass. Hatred, misinformation, and bigotry passing as discussion.

None of us—men, women, children—can afford to let these issues and events slide by. Reflecting upon this whirlwind, I am moved to weigh questions about our bodywork profession's relevance to such powerful, frightening, chaotic and numbingly diverse forces as we observe swirling about us.

In so many of these conflicts between races, ethnic groups, rich and poor, native and immigrant, Christians, Jews, Muslims and the rest, we can discern the same lack of mutual understanding and respect that arises from the same loss of contact—that is with the nitty-gritty humanness and common intimacy that alone can inform all individuals with knowledge of the mutual interdependence that runs so much more deeply than apparent differences and competitive concerns. Mutual understanding and mutual tolerance can be generated only by mutual contact. But instead, as a society we try to retreat into "separate but equal" arrangements, "don't ask, don't tell" contracts, a perverse sort of libertarian mutual neglect, and ultimately create ghettos and erect walled-in "security" communities.

The whole of the European development of the New World was a flight from the atavistic and destructive intolerances of the old regimes, and this flight quickly became a unique religious, social, and finally constitutional attempt to found a new sort of culture that quite self-consciously established a principle of tolerance, among individuals and among groups, so that *all* individuals and groups would be free to develop their enlightened self-interests. This mutual tolerance has always been the primary basis of the Golden Rule, the principle source of all good will among men and women and one of the core values of our constitution.

These were, and are, good values. Exalting them to the level of a national credo and a unique legal constitution that proffers equal opportunity to all persons of all races, classes, and backgrounds was a development of enormous proportions and has been the spiritual as well as the social definition of the New World. In its best moments, it has opened up breathtaking possibilities for the present and future of humanity.

For these reasons, and underscored by these very glimpses of that possible future, the current chronic, habituated, and self-perpetuated pathologies of our collective cultural body are acutely painful, in need of immediate attention. The perversion of the Golden Rule to the Rule of Gold—our "business as usual" had damn well better grip our attention and its symptoms give us a cold sweat, because there is no reason in the world why these pathologies should not eventually be fatal.

The questions for me in the overall context of the bodywork profession are then: Does bodywork have—or perhaps more to the point—*could* it have something to do with evaluating this present situation and discovering possibilities for its remedy? Is it just touchy-feely and largely irrelevant to the compelling social problems that surround us? Or can it somehow be one way towards touching and feeling those very things that may prove to be most largely relevant? We think of ourselves as a caring profession. About what are we most obliged to care? What exactly is it that we should be trying to touch?

Learning about the scope and depth of the physiological and psychological powers of touch—and the devastating consequences of its absence—has given me more of a clue about our current national dilemmas than all of the polls, commentaries, social studies, and political agendas combined. Many repeated and corroborated clinical studies have demonstrated that when laboratory animals have been isolated from contact during their development, they display paranoia, apathy towards their environment, hostility towards new stimulation, stress-related disease profiles, poor mating and parenting instincts, and withdrawal from normal interactions of all kinds. When human children suffer touch deprivation they grow up with subnormal physical development, immune deficiencies, impaired cognitive faculties, and a wide range of emotional disturbances. When a significant part of the contact they do receive has been abusive, with little or no positive intervention available to heal their developmental wounds, they are very frequently overwhelmed by their conditioned urges to perpetuate that abuse on those around them. Does any of this sound at all familiar?

On the other hand, nothing in my adult experience has taught me a fraction as much about meaningful personal interaction, appropriate intimacy, healthy boundaries, tolerance, and conflict resolution as has receiving and giving bodywork. My early massage experiences, training, and practice healed gaps in my frayed personal structure that I had not even been aware of until compassionate touch knit them back together. Nothing else in my life so directly and powerfully addressed my jumble of hurts, numbnesses, disappointments, fears confusion, anger, and self-undermining behaviors which had made me work so hard for so long to learn how to compensate.

Not that the repairs, as welcome as they were, were immediate or easy. I now often smile inwardly at clients who expect to encounter nothing but pleasure and passive relaxation, or at students who think that the work will be a breeze, that their biggest problem will be drumming up a practice. Real and sustained touching is an immediate and pressing engagement in a process towards solutions, not a magic wand or any easy job. But for a person or for a culture that is seriously out of touch, that engagement is everything.

When I first began my professional practice at Esalen in 1974, I had little preparation for the new project I was undertaking and all I knew was that I didn't know how much about it I didn't know. So I made myself a mental rule: Anyone who walked into my work room with a receipt from the office was my next job, no matter what. Every one of them had been sent to teach me something, and I didn't even know yet which ones were going to be the important lessons.

Consequently I ended up in an hour and a half of skin-to-skin intimacy with many people with whom I would not under any other circumstances have had lunch. Some of these encounters were easy enough, some merely tolerable, and some frankly made my flesh crawl. And a good number in the latter category, of course, had a way of enjoying it and coming back for more (isn't it just the people who *nobody* would really want to touch who somehow need it the most?).

Anyway, I stuck to my rule. And I struggled with my personal revulsions and withdrawals so that I might learn my lessons. Sometimes I would just close my eyes; and sometimes even that didn't stop a cold sweat. I would get headaches, or bouts of nausea. Several times I even had to leave the room while they were turning over for the second half of the session, throw up in the lavatory, wash my face with cold water, take ten deep breaths, and go back and finish. I encountered body odors I had not even known existed. I coped with clients' emotional releases no one had told me to get ready for, with all their tears and rages and vomit. I was propositioned and clutched at by both men and women. I was a confidante for problems I didn't even want to know about. And often enough I had to face the disappointment of those who wanted more than I knew how to give.

But eventually, I learned which ones were the important lessons: They *all* were. I had not struggled with my revulsions in order to sort out something else. The nature of that struggle and revulsion were exactly what I was there to learn about. I was there to discover that you could in fact give a great deal to someone you wouldn't want to have lunch with, and that moments of deep gratification and even beauty are always lurking somewhere underneath the most negative of first impressions. And in fact it was the worst of my experiences that were there to teach me that underneath everyone's personality is their *humanity*, and that in the midst of all the eyesores, smells, and neuroses are the real and urgent needs of a lonely creature, and the miracle of life. And somewhere further underneath all of that was my *self*.

In the middle of all these experiences, I met the teacher with whom I would stay for a long time—Dr. Milton Trager. He was the first one to make me know at what depth and with what healing power touch could reach into the most helpless and intractable conditions (not the first to discover it, to be sure, but the first to show me personally at such close quarters). What I saw, and still see in him was someone fearless—even eager—in the face of misery, isolation, and pathology, and someone undaunted in the face of ignorance and apathy. I understood that these observable qualities were the effective antidote for my own squeamishness and fear. And I saw that on a much larger front they were perhaps the only ready means available for confronting the self-induced impotence all around us that hides behind words like "incurable," "unchangeable," and "inevitable."

Educated touch is immediate and direct engagement, contact with the palpable essence of living reality, a concrete combination of flesh and consciousness that creates a medium for the development of creative physical improvements and the possibility of a path through the fear, the confusion, and the nonsense. It is what E.M. Forster meant when he offered his final dictum: "Only connect." It is what Jesus meant when he claimed that "God is love" and what the Buddha meant when he taught that the inevitability of human suffering is only an illusion.

What I further came to realize while learning about bodywork from Dr. Trager was that in order to do more of what I saw him doing I had to learn to *be* more like him, and to be more like him I definitely had to change. Those changes are certainly still in progress, and humblingly slow, but through the ones I have managed to accomplish I have learned just how much change is possible, and how much of it involves reevaluating and revamping the very things we have come to think cannot be altered: character structure, beliefs, reflexes, perception, reality itself as we have learned to know it.

Dr. Trager, and other inspirational leaders and healers I have come to see in this light, have taught me to dare to have a dream. My dream is a personal and social and spiritual vision of humanity based upon the sturdy biological and ecological truths that make life tick and grow. It is of a world in which we face together, touching and connected, the problems common to us all, using together the evolutionary strengths and strategies we have through millennia of evolution come to share. It is of a human race that recognizes the global universality of each of our intensely individual developmental needs.

For even though we have different gods, heroes, and histories, we all have very much the same kind of bodies. We may all view it differently, but we have all done precisely the same thing: We have survived, we have gotten here. And each and every one of us has a piece of the truth of how that was done, and how it can continue. We are a *species*, not a race or a nationality, a political or an ethnic group, or a class; and as members of that species each one of us carries deep within our cells the codes of its past and future success. In this collective enterprise—and no one of us could possibly sustain ourselves alone—our apparent diversity is dwarfed by our essential sameness. It is in fact the genetic richness of that sameness which allows us to develop so differently, and if we manage to forget that our species will be an endangered, or an extinct one.

Black, white, brown, fat, male, female, disabled, rich, poor, white color or blue collar worker, academic, uneducated, elite, disenfranchised, conservative, liberal, old, young, immigrant, native, Christian, Jew, Muslim, whatever—if we choose to use superficial differences as categorical definitives then we are each and every one of us a member of an isolated minority. And there is simply no end to the conflicts we can devise if we so define ourselves.

Truly successful self-interest must always learn to acknowledge this larger Self. And I do believe that bodywork is a way to get in touch with it. A great deal may in fact be up to us.

About the Author

Deane Juhan was born in 1945 in Glenwood Springs, Colorado, and educated at the University of Colorado (BA), the University of Michigan (MA), and the University of California at Berkeley (three and a half years as a doctoral candidate in English literature specializing in William Blake). In 1973 an experience with bodywork at Esalen Institute in Big Sur led to a sudden change in career. Joining the staff at Esalen as bodyworker and instructor (where he remained until 1990), he saw dramatic improvements in a wide variety of conditions as a result of hands-on work and movement reeducation. This quickened his interest in clinical research, and years of study of the physiology of touch and its concrete effects on development, adaptation, skill learning, and healing eventually produced *Job's Body: A Handbook for Bodywork*, as well as the essays in his latest book, *Touched by the Goddess: The Physical, Psychological, and Spiritual Powers of Bodywork*. He is currently a practitioner of the Trager Approach® and an instructor at the Trager Institute, and has developed a series of seminars for all varieties of bodyworkers and therapists, which he presents throughout the United States, Canada, Europe, and Japan.

Also available from
Barrytown/Station Hill

Job's Body
A HANDBOOK FOR BODYWORK
DEANE JUHAN
Expanded Edition

Possibly the most famous and widely used single resource in
the field of bodywork (required for national certification in
massage therapy), this beautifully written book gives a richly
detailed picture of how and why the body responds to therapeutic touch. A reader-friendly yet scientifically reliable and
detailed introduction to the human body, this updated edition
(including new introductory and supplemental material)
surveys "bodywork," showing how its practices alter deep-
seated patterns of body and mind. For general reader as much
as professional and student interested in the body-mind and
not wanting a dry, clinical presentation, this is the book.

TRADE PAPERBACK, $34.95, 450 PAGES, 7 X 10
ISBN: 1-58177-022-7 INDEX, PHOTOGRAPHS, DRAWINGS